Dr. Seuss
(Theodor Geisel)
Second Edition

WHO WROTE THAT?

LOUISA MAY ALCOTT,
SECOND EDITION

JANE AUSTEN

AVI

L. FRANK BAUM

JUDY BLUME,
SECOND EDITION

RAY BRADBURY

BETSY BYARS

MEG CABOT

BEVERLY CLEARY

ROBERT CORMIER

BRUCE COVILLE

SHARON CREECH

ROALD DAHL

CHARLES DICKENS

DR. SEUSS,
SECOND EDITION

ERNEST J. GAINES

S.E. HINTON

WILL HOBBS

ANTHONY HOROWITZ

STEPHEN KING

URSULA K. LE GUIN

MADELEINE L'ENGLE

GAIL CARSON LEVINE

C.S. LEWIS,
SECOND EDITION

LOIS LOWRY

ANN M. MARTIN

STEPHENIE MEYER

L.M. MONTGOMERY

PAT MORA

WALTER DEAN MYERS

ANDRE NORTON

SCOTT O'DELL

CHRISTOPHER PAOLINI

BARBARA PARK

KATHERINE PATERSON

GARY PAULSEN

RICHARD PECK

TAMORA PIERCE

DAVID "DAV" PILKEY

EDGAR ALLAN POE

BEATRIX POTTER

PHILIP PULLMAN

MYTHMAKER:
THE STORY OF
J.K. ROWLING,
SECOND EDITION

MAURICE SENDAK

SHEL SILVERSTEIN

LEMONY SNICKET

GARY SOTO

JERRY SPINELLI

R.L. STINE

EDWARD L.
STRATEMEYER

MARK TWAIN

H.G. WELLS

E.B. WHITE

LAURA INGALLS
WILDER

JACQUELINE WILSON

LAURENCE YEP

JANE YOLEN

Dr. Seuss
(Theodor Geisel)
Second Edition

Tanya Anderson

Foreword by
Kyle Zimmer

CHELSEA HOUSE
An Infobase Learning Company

Dr. Seuss (Theodor Geisel), Second Edition

Copyright © 2011 by Infobase Learning

Chelsea House
An imprint of Infobase Learning
132 West 31st Street
New York, NY 10001

Library of Congress Cataloging-in-Publication Data
Anderson, Tanya.
Dr. Seuss (Theodor Geisel) / by Tanya Anderson. — 2nd ed.
p. cm. — (Who wrote that?)
Includes bibliographical references and index.
ISBN 978-1-60413-750-7 (hardcover)
1. Seuss, Dr.—Juvenile literature. 2. Authors, American—20th century—
Biography—Juvenile literature. 3. Illustrators—United States—Biography—Juvenile
literature. 4. Children's literature—Authorship—Juvenile literature. I. Title. II. Series.
PS3513.E2Z56 2011
813'.52—dc22
[B]   2010030589

Text design by Keith Trego
Cover design by Alicia Post
Composition by EJB Publishing Services
Cover printed by Yurchak Printing, Landisville, Pa.
Book printed and bound by Yurchak Printing, Landisville, Pa.
Date printed: April 2011
Printed in the United States of America

10 9 8 7 6 5 4 3 2 1

Table of Contents

FOREWORD BY
KYLE ZIMMER
PRESIDENT, FIRST BOOK

HUMANITY IS POWERED by stories. From our earliest days as thinking beings, we employed every available tool to tell each other stories. We danced, drew pictures on the walls of our caves, spoke, and sang. All of this extraordinary effort was designed to entertain, recount the news of the day, explain natural occurrences—and then gradually to build religious and cultural traditions and establish the common bonds and continuity that eventually formed civilizations. Stories are the most powerful force in the universe; they are the primary element that has distinguished our evolutionary path.

Our love of the story has not diminished with time. Enormous segments of societies are devoted to the art of storytelling. Book sales in the United States alone topped $24 billion in 2006; movie studios spend fortunes to create and promote stories; and the news industry is more pervasive in its presence than ever before.

There is no mystery to our fascination. Great stories are magic. They can introduce us to new cultures, or remind us of the nobility and failures of our own, inspire us to greatness or scare us to death; but above all, stories provide human insight on a level that is unavailable through any other source. In fact, stories connect each of us to the rest of humanity not just in our own time, but also throughout history.

This special magic of books is the greatest treasure that we can hand down from generation to generation. In fact, that spark in a child that comes from books became the motivation for the creation of my organization, First Book, a national literacy program with a simple mission: to provide new books to the most disadvantaged children. At present, First Book has been at work in hundreds of communities for over a decade. Every year children in need receive millions of books through our organization and millions more are provided through dedicated literacy institutions across the United States and around the world. In addition, groups of people dedicate themselves tirelessly to working with children to share reading and stories in every imaginable setting from schools to the streets. Of course, this Herculean effort serves many important goals. Literacy translates to productivity and employability in life and many other valid and even essential elements. But at the heart of this movement are people who love stories, love to read, and want desperately to ensure that no one misses the wonderful possibilities that reading provides.

When thinking about the importance of books, there is an overwhelming urge to cite the literary devotion of great minds. Some have written of the magnitude of the importance of literature. Amy Lowell, an American poet, captured the concept when she said, "Books are more than books. They are the life, the very heart and core of ages past, the reason why men lived and worked and died, the essence and quintessence of their lives." Others have spoken of their personal obsession with books, as in Thomas Jefferson's simple statement: "I live for books." But more compelling, perhaps, is the almost instinctive excitement in children for books and stories.

Throughout my years at First Book, I have heard truly extraordinary stories about the power of books in the lives of children. In one case, a homeless child, who had been bounced from one location to another, later resurfaced— and the only possession that he had fought to keep was the book he was given as part of a First Book distribution months earlier. More recently, I met a child who, upon receiving the book he wanted, flashed a big smile and said, "This is my big chance!" These snapshots reveal the true power of books and stories to give hope and change lives.

As these children grow up and continue to develop their love of reading, they will owe a profound debt to those volunteers who reached out to them—a debt that they may repay by reaching out to spark the next generation of readers. But there is a greater debt owed by all of us—a debt to the storytellers, the authors, who have bound us together, inspired our leaders, fueled our civilizations, and helped us put our children to sleep with their heads full of images and ideas.

WHO WROTE THAT? is a series of books dedicated to introducing us to a few of these incredible individuals. While we have almost always honored stories, we have not uniformly honored storytellers. In fact, some of the most important authors have toiled in complete obscurity throughout their lives or have been openly persecuted for the uncomfortable truths that they have laid before us. When confronted with the magnitude of their written work or perhaps the daily grind of our own, we can forget that writers are people. They struggle through the same daily indignities and dental appointments, and they experience the intense joy and bottomless despair that many of us do. Yet somehow they rise above it all to deliver a powerful thread that connects us all. It is a rare honor to have the opportunity that these books provide to share the lives of these extraordinary people. Enjoy.

Children's book writer and illustrator Theodor Seuss Geisel in June 1955.
As Dr. Seuss, Geisel became one of the most famous children's authors and
illustrators of all time. His lucky break came when, after being rejected by 27
publishers, he accidently ran into a fellow Dartmouth College classmate (who
worked for a publisher) on the street in New York City.

1

To Think That It Happened on Madison Avenue

FEW COUPLES HAD traveled as extensively as Ted and Helen Geisel in their first nine years of marriage. Ted, born Theodor Seuss Geisel, was 32 years old in 1936, and he was restless. He had found considerable success in his advertising career, but somehow still felt that he was not doing what made him happiest. Enormously talented as both a writer and illustrator, Ted was in demand to create catchy ads that attracted consumers to buy such things as bug spray, bags of sugar, and automobiles. He was also successful in drawing cartoons for adults. Frequent travel to Europe was possible because of his successes. Ted and Helen enjoyed these trips, and Ted found that exploring other countries boosted his creativity.

The Geisels boarded the Swedish luxury liner MS *Kungsholm* in New York Harbor and headed for Europe

Did you know...

The Olympic Summer Games of 1936 were loaded with tension. Berlin was chosen as the site for the 1936 Games in 1931, before Adolf Hitler and his Nazi Party gained power in Germany. As the games approached, Hitler's belief in a superior Aryan race—Caucasians with blond hair and blue eyes—and his hatred for Jews and quest for power were becoming well known. Many countries considered not sending their athletes at all. Knowing he was on the world stage at last, Hitler dialed back his racism long enough to put the Olympic Committee at ease. Hitler's goal was to outdo any of the previous Olympics by building the most elaborate stadium to date and the first-ever Olympic Village, thereby proving the superiority of Germans. And he almost succeeded.

Germany won more medals in the 1936 Olympics than any other country (89); the United States was second (56). Despite the Germans' success, the most memorable aspect of the games came when African-American Jesse Owens won four gold medals in track and field—a result quite contrary to Hitler's belief in an Aryan super race.

in the summer of 1936. An air of uncertainty traveled with the people on board because rumors of possible German aggression in Europe were growing. World War I had ended in 1918, but the tensions among Germany, France, and England had not diminished over the years. Instead, the rise of the Nazi Party under the leadership of Adolf Hitler in Germany added to Europeans' fears of another war. Geisel, himself a second-generation German American, was interested in national and international issues and therefore kept a keen eye on these events. Regardless, he and Helen had decided to go ahead with their trip, joining other Americans who also had ventured into Europe that summer to attend the Olympic Summer Games in Berlin. The Geisels did not go to Berlin, but they kept up on the news of Jesse Owens's four gold medals as they dined at Swiss cafés.

Geisel enjoyed the Swiss scenery: the pointed mountains, the winding roads, the unusual buses and houses. Here his imagination came alive again. He drew scenes of odd creatures hanging from dangerous peaks or wandering up long, crooked paths. Just for fun, he learned to yodel. Helen, ever his encourager, suggested he keep practicing, but only in the shower.

By the time their holiday was nearly over, the threat of invasion by Hitler was more imminent. Geisel was concerned about his grandfather's homeland, and indeed all of Europe, and he told Helen that perhaps it was time for him to get serious about his own life. She knew that it was her husband's deepest longing to write and draw his own children's books. Even though he had enjoyed illustrating someone else's stories a few years earlier (a book called *Boners* in 1931), Helen suggested that he should go ahead and try his hand at writing his own children's book. Geisel agreed.

IT BEGAN WITH A BEAT

The Geisels boarded the MS *Kungsholm* eager to return home with a new plan in mind. They had been aboard for only eight days, however, when a powerful storm pounded the ship. Helen stayed in her cabin during the worst hours, but Ted grew anxious and needed to move around. He held on tightly to the rails as he walked the deck, but eventually gave up his pacing and sat down at the ship's bar. There he picked up some of the ship's stationery and began to write. The rhythm of the ship's engines ran through his mind, over and over again, and the mixture of the incessant beat and the bouncy ride on rough seas made concentration difficult. To settle his mind, he began to recite lines from "'Twas the Night Before Christmas," which, oddly enough, seemed to match the rhythm of the engine sounds. Then, according to Judith and Neil Morgan's biography, *Dr. Seuss and Mr. Geisel*, seemingly from nowhere, Ted heard and spoke the line, "And that is a story that no one can beat, and to think that I saw it on Mulberry Street." Mulberry Street was, in fact, a real street in his hometown of Springfield, Massachusetts.

Even after the Geisels had returned to their home, the young writer could not get the rhythm out of his head. In order to get it to stop, Ted decided to go ahead and write an entire story using that maddening rhythm. If nothing else, perhaps the sounds would go away.

Like most writers, Geisel found that creating the "just right" words for his story was not easy. He wrote, rewrote, and kept rewriting the manuscript, always critical of his own choice of words. More than anything, he wanted to write and illustrate a book that would make children want "to turn page after page," as he told Helen, according to the Morgan biography. He drew illustrations to help fill out the story, making creatures and scenes that would delight and could, all by themselves, tell the story. Although some writers in the 1930s preferred to use a typewriter when writing a manuscript, Ted preferred to print with pencil on yellow paper. Six months after beginning, Ted completed the book he entitled *A Story That No One Can Beat*, a book filled with odd creatures and characters creating their own parade on Mulberry Street.

THE RIGHT PLACE AT THE RIGHT TIME

Today when a writer or illustrator wants to submit something to a publisher, he or she usually will use e-mail, the U.S. mail, or another delivery service to send the material. In the 1930s and 1940s, however, it was not unusual for people to hand-deliver their manuscripts or drawings from publisher to publisher in New York City. That is exactly what Ted Geisel did. During the winter of 1936–1937, he showed his book to 27 different publishers. One after another, they rejected *A Story That No One Can Beat*, often commenting that it was "too different" from the kinds of children's books being developed at the time. Few rhyming books were being published, and the odd illustrations Geisel had drawn were even more atypical. Some publishers even complained that his story had no moral or lesson for the child. The young author was especially upset about that criticism. He had not intended to preach to children; instead, he merely had wanted to give them something fun to read.

The twenty-seventh rejection was the last one for Geisel. Dejected, he shoved the papers under his arm and decided to do two things: to return to his advertising and cartoon work for adults and to burn his only copy of *A Story That No One Can Beat*. He headed for home, walking along Madison Avenue in New York City. Lost in thought, Geisel was surprised to hear his name called by a familiar voice. It was Mike McClintock, a fellow classmate of his from his college years at Dartmouth. Right away, Mike asked him what he had under his arm. Geisel answered that it was a children's book manuscript that he was taking home to burn because no one was interested in publishing it. McClintock smiled at him and pointed at the building in front of which they were standing. Geisel's old friend had just been hired, only three hours previously, as the juvenile book editor at that particular publishing house, Vanguard Press. He

Did you know...

When *And to Think That I Saw It on Mulberry Street!* was published in 1937, the people of Springfield, Massachusetts, were a little concerned. Unsure of what the book was really about, some townspeople were afraid that the book was going to tell personal, even embarrassing, stories about some of them who actually lived on Mulberry Street. Imagine their relief when they finally saw Dr. Seuss's children's book. Instead of a serious, scandalous book, *Mulberry Street* delighted them with tons of funny-looking creatures and a little boy who had a great imagination—a boy not unlike the young Ted Geisel they had known.

invited Geisel to come up to his office so they could take a look at the book he was getting ready to destroy.

Thirty minutes later, Vanguard Press's publisher James Henle agreed to publish the book. The only immediate change he wanted involved the title. Henle felt that the book needed a catchier title in order to sell successfully. Henle was different from most publishers of that time because he was interested in making books that no one else was making yet. He was willing to take some risks by publishing new kinds of books by new authors and illustrators. Geisel's second title was the one that stuck: *And to Think That I Saw It on Mulberry Street!* According to Judith and Neil Morgan's biography, *Dr. Seuss and Mr. Geisel*, Geisel later told people about that lucky day, "If I had been going down the other side of Madison Avenue, I'd be in the dry-cleaning business today." Showing his gratitude, Geisel named the story's narrator "Marco," the name of Mike McClintock's son, and he dedicated the book to Mike's wife, Helene.

ON THE BOOKSHELVES AT LAST

When the book arrived in bookstores in the fall of 1937, James Henle paid for a full-page ad in *Publishers Weekly*, a special magazine for people in the bookselling and publishing business. The ad showed a reindeer pulling a cart down Mulberry Street and read: "Booksellers, hitch on! This is the start of a parade that will take you places!" by "the good Dr. Seuss." Geisel had used the pseudonym "Dr. Seuss" since his college days, and he wanted to continue to use it on his children's books, too. (A pseudonym is a "pen name" some authors use instead of their real name.) He sometimes commented, less-than-seriously, that he was saving his "real" name for his first novel.

The book reviews about *Mulberry Street* were positive from the beginning. Reviewers are people who read new books and write critiques about them for booksellers to use when they need to decide which new books to put on their store shelves. Good reviews usually mean that a book will get more shelf space, and that means the book has a better chance of selling well. One of the first reviews helped establish Dr. Seuss as one of the best children's book authors of his time. According to Morgan, it simply said, "They say it's for children, but better get a copy for yourself and marvel at the good Dr. Seuss' impossible pictures and the moral tale of a little boy who exaggerated." Another reviewer described the book as being a mix of "the funny papers and the tall tale."

Mulberry Street was colorful and expensive to print, but despite the one-dollar cover price (a high price for a children's book of that time), it sold even better than the publisher had expected. Dr. Seuss had landed on bookshelves and in the hearts of adults and children all over the country.

The cobblestoned main street of Springfield, Massachusetts, Theodor Geisel's hometown, in 1903, the year before he was born.

2

Growing Up

THEODOR SEUSS GEISEL was born on March 2, 1904, in Springfield, Massachusetts, to Theodor Robert Geisel and Henrietta Seuss Geisel. From the beginning, his parents called him Ted. Little Ted joined an older sister, Margaretha Christine Geisel, who decided to go by a different name, too. A fun-loving and intelligent girl, she often told people her name was "Marnie Mecca Ding Ding Guy." From that came the name everyone called her: Marnie. Ted, only two years younger, adored her.

At the time of Ted's birth, Springfield, Massachusetts, was already well known for three landmark companies: the Smith

& Wesson gun business; the Milton Bradley game company; and G. & C. Merriam, publishers of the nation's best-known dictionary. The Geisels were among the nearly 1,000 German Americans who lived in Springfield, and Ted's grandfather, who was also named Theodor Geisel, was co-owner of one of the most successful businesses in town, a brewery. Ted's grandfather had immigrated from Mühlhausen, Germany, to the United States, settling in Springfield in 1867, where the Kalmbach and Geisel Brewery opened in 1876. The townspeople nicknamed it the "come back and guzzle" brewery. Both the Geisel family and the Kalmbach family lived beside the business. In 1879, Ted's father was born in Springfield. It was a good city for a growing business and a loving family.

Ted's mother, Henrietta (Nettie) Seuss, also was born and grew up in this town. Her parents had emigrated there from the Bavarian region of Germany, and they pronounced their last name as it had been in Germany: *zoice, not zoos.* The Geisel family business made beer, and the Seuss family business made bread. When the young Theodor Geisel married the baker's daughter, some townspeople made it their business to criticize both families. At the turn of the century, owning a bakery was an admirable business venture, but owning a brewery was not. Concerns over excessive drinking caused political reformers to think that they should make the purchase of alcohol illegal. This idea later turned into the Prohibition movement, a progressive idea supported by those who wanted to stop the production, sale, and distribution of alcohol in the United States.

In 1901, when Ted's parents got married, the Prohibition movement was already well underway. The most vocal group was the Women's Christian Temperance Union. They (and others) believed that drinking alcohol was a special problem in our country, harming individuals, families, and communities. At first, it was up to individual states to pass laws that would make their own state "dry," meaning it was illegal to sell or buy alcohol. (Today, some communities are still "dry.") Eventually, however, reformers wanted the federal government to establish an amendment to the Constitution that would make Prohibition the law of the land. In 1920, the Eighteenth Amendment did just that. For 20 years, between the time Ted's parents married and the passage of the Eighteenth Amendment, the Kalmbach and Geisel Brewery suffered as this movement grew. Eventually it closed and Ted's father had to find new work to support his family.

A CHILDHOOD ON FAIRFIELD STREET

Ted grew up knowing all about the tensions regarding his family's business, but he had a happy childhood nonetheless. Nettie read bedtime stories to her son and daughter, using a soft, rhythmic voice to lull them to sleep. Ted often told others that his mother was the one who had helped set the rhythms in his mind that he used when writing children's books. Nettie Geisel nurtured Ted's love of words by reading books that were imaginative. One of Ted's favorites was *The Hole Book* by Peter Newell. Each page had a hole in it. This was the first book that made Ted think that writing children's books could be fun. His mother also read rhyming books to Ted and Marnie, particularly the Goops books by Gelett Burgess. As Ted grew older, Nettie knew that she could get him to do things he did not really want to do just by promising to buy him a book. Ted agreed to take piano lessons, for example, when he learned he could get books for playing well.

Ted's father was a loving parent, too, and provided the discipline that would be so important in the writer's life. From his father, Ted learned to strive to do the very best he could. The elder Geisel, an expert marksman, held a world title in 1902. He tried to teach his son to shoot, but Ted was not quite as good as his father. Still, he learned what it took to "hit the target," not only in this sport but in his other endeavors as well.

Ted and Marnie loved to play in and around their house on Fairfield Street. The attic held trunks filled with all kinds of clothing. Ted and Marnie would dress up in costumes and pretend to be all kinds of people and things. Ted was especially fond of wearing hats, something he would continue to enjoy to the end of his life. His room was dotted with books, paper, and pencils. Doodling was one of his favorite pastimes. Growing up, the young Geisels could hear the sounds of the animals at the nearby Springfield Zoo, one of their favorite places to visit. Although Ted regularly saw the real animals, when he drew them, they were funny-looking creatures. He often included them in his silly stories and cartoons.

Growing up in Springfield was mostly a wonderful experience for Ted. Two incidents, however, were not pleasant. Another sister, Henrietta, was born in 1906 and died of pneumonia 18 months later. Ted never forgot seeing her tiny casket as it rested in the music room of his house. He also never forgot being locked in a closet by their housekeeper as punishment for "bad behavior." From that time on, Ted was a claustrophobic—afraid of small, enclosed spaces. Even as an adult, he was unable to overcome this fear.

FRIENDS AND FATHER

In 1908, Ted started school. He loved to watch the goings-on along the streets of Springfield: the horse-drawn wagons, the trolley cars, bicycles, and the automobiles that bumped along. Ted played with classmates and earned their friendship because of his easy-going ways. He loved to laugh and to smile, and he told the best stories around. Not very athletic, Ted had other strengths that made him well liked and popular. He was, for instance, the winner of his friends' ear-wiggling contest. Some of these early friends would show up in some of Dr. Seuss's books later. These buddies had some unusual names, like Norval Bacon, and Ted loved to name his characters accordingly. Words were magical to Ted, and he seldom passed up an opportunity to tuck away a word or a name in his memory for later use.

Did you know...

Dr. Seuss made up the names of most of his animal creatures. In fact, he said he had a special dictionary he used to look up the spellings. When it came to naming people in his stories, however, this fun-loving author often used the names of real people he knew or had known. For example, Marco (*And to Think That I Saw It on Mulberry Street!* and *McElligot's Pool*) was named for the son of his publisher, Mike McClintock. The lovable elephant Horton (*Horton Hatches the Egg* and *Horton Hears a Who!*) was named for a classmate at Dartmouth College.

Ted and his father had a close friendship too. When the elder Geisel was appointed to the Springfield Park board in 1909, he began to take Ted on walks through the beautiful park and behind the scenes at the park's centerpiece: the Springfield Zoo. Ted brought along his sketchbook and drew pictures of plants and animals that he saw. Of course, Ted's pictures seldom looked like the real thing, and his sister loved to tease him about his odd drawings. According to the Morgan biography, his father later recalled, "Ted always had a pencil in hand." Just as his mother encouraged Ted's love of words, his father supported Ted's drawing talents. Their mutual love of nature grew, too. In 1910, father and son sat in a field behind their house to wait for the appearance of Halley's Comet, a phenomenon that happens only every 76 years. Of that night, Ted recalled, as quoted by Morgan, "I saw Halley's Comet and my first owl on the same night."

At the end of each workday, Ted waited at the corner for his father, who always brought Ted a copy of the local daily newspaper, the *Boston American*. Ted's favorite part was the comic page, and his favorite comic strip was *Krazy Kat*. The two Geisel men especially enjoyed spending time in the workshop Ted's father had set up. Together they tinkered and invented things, such as a "biceps-strengthening machine." Ted loved to see other Springfielders' inventions, too, and he copied advertisements he saw in the newspaper of such inventions as a new coal stove with a complex maze of compartments. Ted loved things that had intricate looping sections or wild, winding stairs. These kinds of objects, too, eventually found their way into his books.

HISTORY AND HERITAGE

Ted recalled many historical events that took place when he lived in Springfield. He was 10 years old when he saw the headlines announcing the sinking of the RMS *Titanic*, a luxury ocean liner on its maiden voyage. He wrote a poem about the event. He was excited to read about the opening of the Panama Canal in 1914, which joins the Atlantic Ocean and the Pacific Ocean. Reading about it made Ted eager to travel. This remarkable man-made canal across Central America allows ships to cut across the middle of the Western Hemisphere rather than having to travel all the way around the southernmost tip of South America.

Travel was on the minds of Ted's parents when they decided to travel by train to San Francisco to attend the 1915 World's Fair. Ted's father made his family proud when he took part in a demonstration at one of the fair's booths. The operators of the booth invited him to call any city in the country. Few places had telephones in 1915, and transcontinental phone calls were practically unheard of. So Ted's father called the mayor of Springfield, Massachusetts! Ted never forgot the headlines in the next day's newspaper: GEISEL CALLS MAYOR.

Ted grew up knowing and appreciating his German heritage. He and Marnie spoke German before they spoke English. They sang Christmas songs in their grandparents' native language and practiced German traditions. Like many Americans of their era, the Geisels were closely connected to their European cultures and proud of them. But the mood of the country was changing. Eleven-year-old Ted was shocked along with the rest of America to hear of the German torpedo attack against the British ocean liner RMS *Lusitania* in 1915. The ship sank, and nearly 1,200 died, of whom 128 were Americans.

Even in small towns like Springfield, German Americans suffered insults and cold stares. As World War I (1914–1918) drew near, Ted could see the changes around

The 1915 sinking of the RMS Lusitania, on which 120 Americans died, was caused by a German torpedo attack. It also aroused suspicion of German Americans, like the Geisel family, in the United States.

him, but he did not understand people's prejudices. He did not want to be treated like a lesser person because of his heritage. Although it hurt him to see fellow German Americans come under suspicion, Ted covered his concern and pain with his ready smile and outgoing sense of humor.

Ted turned 13 in 1917, and the country was entering a new time, too. Not only was Prohibition on the horizon—and with it the certainty that the Geisels' business would have to close—but it was also becoming clear that the United States would soon be joining the war in Europe. Many German Americans had mixed feelings about this. They loved their homeland, but they valued their new home here, too. In April 1917, the German navy attacked Ameri-

Did you know...

PROHIBITION AND THE BREWERY BUSINESS

It is possible that if beer had not become the most popular alcoholic drink in America, the Eighteenth Amendment might never have happened. When German immigrants began arriving in great numbers in the late nineteenth century, they brought beer—and the know-how to produce it—with them. In 1895, the largest brewery in America was Pabst in Milwaukee, followed by Anheuser-Busch in St. Louis. Smaller breweries sprang up in cities across the country as well, serving their local regions and meeting the growing demand for beer.

With this demand came the growth of saloons, where a person could buy liquor or beer by the glass. So many saloons were built in the 1890s that, in some cities, you could find a saloon for every 150 to 200 residents. Because of the increased competition, saloon owners began to offer free lunches and even some "vices," such as gambling, cock-fighting, and prostitution, in order to bring in more customers. The saloons themselves were unattractive and tended to draw the "less respectable" people in the area.

Concerned citizens formed the Anti-Saloon League, which only strengthened a growing anti-alcohol, or Prohibition, movement. The movement grew so strong that politicians paid attention, and in 1919, the Eighteenth Amendment, also known as the Volstead Act, was passed, making it illegal to manufacture, sell, or transport alcohol. Most small breweries went out of business. In 1933, the amendment was repealed with the Twenty-first Amendment.

can ships on the seas, and President Woodrow Wilson got the approval of the U.S. Congress to declare war on Germany. From this point on, the Geisels knew that thinking of themselves as German American was not wise.

Indeed, the Geisel clan was an American family, actively involved on the home front in providing support for the war effort. Ted's mother and sister knitted socks and afghans for the troops. Ted joined his fellow Boy Scouts and sold Liberty Bonds, a form of financing that provided a major source of income to the government during the war. In fact, he sold so many that he was among a group of Boy Scouts to receive a medal from former president Theodore Roosevelt in 1918. Sadly, this event turned out to be a disappointment for 14-year-old Ted. When the former president had handed out the last medal, Ted stood alone, still waiting for his. Someone had made a mistake and had ordered 9 medals instead of 10. Ted felt foolish and embarrassed as Roosevelt bellowed, "What are you doing here?" Ted had no answer and was shoved offstage. From that moment, Ted Geisel had a fear of making public appearances.

DISAPPOINTMENTS LEAD TO DETERMINATION

When the war ended in November 1918, Ted was a sophomore at Central High School. Ted took his only formal art class there and soon transferred out. He was frustrated by all the rules the art teacher imposed about the "right way" to draw things. Later, the man who would be known as Dr. Seuss said, according to Maryann N. Weidt in *Oh, The Places He Went: A Story About Dr. Seuss*: "I was free forever from art-by-the-rule books. . . . That teacher wanted me to draw the world as it is, and I wanted to draw things as I saw them." The teacher's suggestion that Ted consider finding another career besides art only made the young man more determined someday to make his living as an artist. In his other classes, Ted was a B-student, except in math, which was very hard for him.

He enjoyed school, especially the extracurricular activities, and found a place for his humor, writing, and drawing skills at *The Recorder*, the school's weekly newspaper. Ted drew cartoons and wrote humorous one-liners, poems, and satires, usually under the pseudonym T.S. LeSieg (Geisel spelled backward). As a senior, he was joke editor of the yearbook, had a part in the senior play, and was secretary of the student senate. His class voted him Class Artist and Class Wit.

Of all his teachers at Central High School, only one saw how truly talented Ted Geisel was. Edwin "Red" Smith was a recent graduate of Dartmouth and became Ted's English teacher at CHS. This teacher made Ted believe that he really could make a living as a writer and illustrator. Mr. Smith encouraged Ted to apply to Dartmouth, where many of Ted's classmates were headed, and he wrote a letter of recommendation that secured Ted's acceptance to the university. In June 1921, Theodor Seuss Geisel graduated high school and looked forward to his college years at Dartmouth.

An exterior view of Dartmouth College in Hanover, New Hampshire. When Ted Geisel attended the college in the 1920s, he began writing and illustrating for various school publications.

3

The Grad Becomes an Ad Man

IN 1921, TED GEISEL started college at Dartmouth in Hanover, New Hampshire. The new decade brought the Geisel family some difficult financial times. When Prohibition finally was passed as the Eighteenth Amendment in 1920, the family-owned brewery had to be shut down. His grandfather had passed away during Geisel's senior year of high school, so his father had become president of the brewery. With the brewery closed (and unlikely to ever be reopened), his father had to look for other work. During Geisel's college years, his father found some success in the real estate business. He also continued to serve on the park's board, but without any income. Thankfully, an inheritance from his grandfather made it possible for Geisel to continue with his plans for a college education.

THE DARTMOUTH YEARS

Geisel wanted to major in English. He loved writing and literature and looked forward to his classes. During his first semester at Dartmouth, he wanted to write and draw for the college's literary-arts magazine, *Jack-O-Lantern*. The first issue of his freshman year contained four of his illustrations. *Jacko*, as the students called it, became Geisel's passion, much more than his classes. He drew cartoons, including many with cats, and usually signed them "Ted G." His writing often consisted of puns housed in funny one-liners as captions. In his first semester, he was elected treasurer of the freshman class and became an art editor for the freshman publication, *Green Book*.

Geisel always wore a bow tie, which became his trademark for the rest of his life. Classmates saw a young man who always smiled, often joked, and was never unkind toward anyone. "You never heard him grump," said one classmate, according to the Morgan biography of Geisel.

Geisel also enjoyed taking classes in German and German literature. Some of his other favorite classes included botany (the study of plants), zoology (the study of animals), and the psychology of advertising. In this class, he learned which colors people pay the most attention to, such as red. All of those classes would prove useful later when he began working on children's books. Geisel usually carried a sketchbook to class so he could draw. He drew plants and animals, but he seldom stopped there. Some objects looked "normal," but many were more than a little unusual. Once he drew a picture of his zoology professor's dog, a beagle named Spot. It was a good likeness of Spot, except that Geisel had drawn the dog with antlers coming out of his head. Would this creature later reappear as the Grinch's best friend, Max?

Geisel continued to write and draw for *Jacko*. Many students and faculty recognized his work, making him quite popular. As a sophomore and a junior, he spent most of his time at *Jacko*'s office. His editor-in-chief at the publication was a young man named Norman Maclean, who later wrote the acclaimed story collection, *A River Runs Through It and Other Stories* (1976). Here, surrounded by some of the school's best writers, Geisel learned how to make words and pictures work together to say something—something silly or something important. He also learned to use pseudonyms to keep some people from knowing which cartoons he had drawn. Some of these made-up names included Sing Sing Prison, L. Burbank, and Seuss. Geisel himself became editor-in-chief of *Jacko* his senior year.

As graduation day approached, Geisel decided he wanted to attend Oxford University in England. Knowing his family did not have the money to pay for such a costly education, Geisel applied for a fellowship—a kind of scholarship for graduate school. Before even learning if he had been awarded it or not, Geisel exaggerated by telling his father that the fellowship was his. The next day, after his proud father had shared the news with the editor of the town's newspaper, everyone read the *Springfield Union*'s headline: GEISEL WINS SCHOLARSHIP TO GO TO OXFORD.

Unfortunately, Geisel did not get the fellowship. He waited until graduation day from Dartmouth to tell his father the bad news. Though angry, his father told him that since the newspaper had reported that Geisel was going to go to Oxford, the family just would have to make a way.

During the summer between his years at Dartmouth and graduate school at Oxford, Geisel worked as a replacement columnist at the *Springfield Union*. He wrote some comical articles that again relied on his hallmark puns and clever humor. His time at the newspaper ended after he wrote an unflattering review of a play. His summer was nearly over anyway, because in August 1925, Geisel sailed for England.

OFF TO OXFORD

Geisel's stay at Oxford was short, but memorable. While there, he at first thought he wanted to become a professor of English literature, but after only a few classes, Geisel

Did you know...

Some very famous people—from scientists to writers, politicians to comedians—attended Oxford University in London, England. Among them are:

Bill Clinton, former U.S. president

Stephen Hawking, physicist

King Abdullah II of Jordan

Rowan Atkinson, comedian and actor

Tony Blair, former prime minister of the United Kingdom

C.S. Lewis, author of the Narnia series

J.R.R. Tolkien, author of *The Hobbit* and *The Lord of the Rings*

Edwin Hubble, astronomer

Michael Rosen, children's novelist and poet

Lewis Carroll (Charles Dodgson), author of *Alice's Adventures in Wonderland* realized that he did not want to teach. World War I had ended only a few years earlier, and Geisel's German ancestry made him feel as if he were an outsider. He found other "outsiders" to socialize with. His humorous writings and never-ending sketches kept him company, too. Geisel bordered his literature notes with characters that would someday be famous. One of his new friends, an American girl named Helen Marion Palmer, watched as he doodled in class. She loved his illustrations and told him, as quoted in Morgan, "You're crazy to be a professor. What you really want to do is draw." About the two students, Geisel later said, again according to Morgan, "You never saw a better case of love at first sight." Helen especially liked his drawing of a flying cow. Geisel and his encouraging classmate became inseparable, and often rode together on a motorcycle with a sidecar. During one trip, Geisel accidentally ran off the road, and he and Helen ended up in a ditch. They were unharmed, but Geisel took that opportunity to ask Helen to marry him. Picking grass from her hair, she accepted.

Although Geisel was happy with Helen as his fiancée, he was not happy with Oxford. One of his college advisors suggested he leave the classroom and travel through Europe instead. That would be an education all its own. Helen finished her master's degree and planned to return to America to teach English. In 1926, after her schooling was over, she did just that. Geisel spent the summer touring Europe with his family, who had come to visit him. The Geisels traveled in England, France, Switzerland, and Germany, where they visited his mother's family's hometown of Mülhausen.

After his parents and Marnie returned to Massachusetts, Geisel went back to Paris to study. Soon the young man realized he did not know enough French to understand what his teachers were saying. While in Paris, Geisel saw a few well-known American writers, including Ernest Hemingway. He recalled, as stated in Morgan, "I was scared . . . to walk over and ask him [what he was writing] lest he ask me what *I* was writing. I was a twenty-two-year-old kid writing knock-kneed limericks about goats and geese and other stuff that I couldn't sell. He was probably writing *A Farewell to Arms*."

Realizing that his formal education was over, Geisel got on a boat and went to the island of Corsica, off the coast of France. He painted pictures of donkeys for a month. When he felt his drawing was not going well, he tried writing again. He even tried to write a novel in Italian—and he knew even less Italian than he knew French. "I couldn't understand a word of it," he later said, according to Weidt. Geisel did not waste his creativity, though. He turned the entire experience into one two-line cartoon.

BACK IN THE U.S.A.

In February 1927, Geisel returned home to the United States, after spending a year and a half in Europe. Helen had already arrived a month earlier to accept a teaching position in Orange, New Jersey, not far from New York City. When Geisel's ship docked in New York's harbor, Helen met him there. Geisel had no job leads, so their marriage plans would have to wait. After a nice dinner, he said good-bye to Helen as he boarded a train for Springfield to join his family.

Eager to get a start as a freelance writer and illustrator, Geisel set up an office at his Fairfield Street home. He sent off dozens of cartoons and humorous writings to publishers in New York, hoping one of them would buy his work or offer him a job. Odd-looking animals and unrecognizable creatures appeared, as usual, in his cartoons.

Ted and Helen Geisel outside their home in La Jolla, California, in April 1957. The couple met at the University of Oxford and married in 1927.

February passed, then March, and then April with no positive responses. Only slightly discouraged, Geisel checked into a hotel in New York so he could show his work in person. Helen kept encouraging him and told people about Geisel's wonderful animals. Still, a week later, Geisel had not sold a single thing, so he returned to Springfield. A staff job was not forthcoming, that was a certainty. Geisel drifted in and out of some "funks and depressions," as he called them, according to the Morgan biography, but turned his moods into silliness as he created more and more cartoons. This became a pattern of his throughout his life.

Geisel started to draw hysterical political cartoons, making fun of some of New York's and Chicago's best-known citizens and leaders. He sent those and other pieces to some of the most popular magazines of the era, including *Life*, *The Saturday Evening Post*, and *The New Yorker* in particular. May passed, then June. July brought more than warmth and sunshine—it also brought Geisel a letter from *The Saturday Evening Post*. Inside was an acceptance letter and a check for $25 for one of his cartoons. The cartoon, featuring the wildly popular Lawrence of Arabia, appeared in the July 16, 1927, issue. Geisel simply signed it "Seuss." The editors thought that pseudonym was fine, but added, according to Morgan, in smaller type beneath, "Drawn by Theodor Seuss Geisel." It was his first broadly published work.

Typically optimistic, Geisel took his life savings of $1,000 and left Springfield for New York City. He and John Rose, a former staff member of *Jack-O-Lantern*, roomed together in a rat-infested apartment in Greenwich Village. His roommate knew an editor at a well-known humor magazine, *Judge*. (This type of magazine, known as a "smart magazine," was popular with the elite class because it offered entertainment in the form of satire and cartoons that poked fun at subjects the rich found amusing.) John set Geisel up with an interview there. After one interview, Geisel was offered a staff position making $75 a week.

Once again, Geisel's positive outlook paid off. Now that he had a good job, Geisel was ready to marry Helen, but they had to wait for a time. First, they had to wait for the birth of Geisel's niece. His sister Marnie gave birth to

Peggy on November 1, 1927. She became one of Geisel's greatest delights. Little Peggy attended Geisel and Helen's wedding on November 29, along with about 40 other family members and friends. Geisel was 23; his bride was 29.

MAGAZINES AND ADVERTISING

Geisel's work at *Judge* went well, but competition for readers and advertising was strong. *The New Yorker, Judge*'s fiercest competitor, sold more copies as time went by, and was able to pull some of *Judge*'s advertising accounts away. As a result, Geisel's salary was reduced to $50 a week. Sometimes he received free "stuff" instead of money when things got really tight at the magazine. For example, one week Geisel's salary was 1,872 Little Gem Nail Clippers, care of the company that advertised them in the magazine.

Did you know...

Magazines and newspapers depend on selling advertisements for their survival—something that is as true today as it was during Ted Geisel's years as an "ad man." In the 1920s and 1930s, before television, most ads were in print or on the radio. When buying advertising space in a magazine, a company would decide which magazine to use based on its circulation or on the number of copies sold. (The more copies that were sold, the more exposure the ad would get.) Think of how that works today with television: Because the Super Bowl has so many millions of viewers, a single 30-second commercial costs more than $2 million!

Another time he received 100 cans of Barbasol shaving cream. According to the Morgan biography, Geisel took it in stride: "I sort of loved trading my stuff for their stuff. I was happier in one way under the barter system than I've ever been since. When you get paid in money, it leads to accountants and lawyers."

Not only was he published in *Judge*, but he also sold work (for real money) to *Life*, *Redbook*, and *Vanity Fair*. During this time, Geisel began using the pseudonym "Dr. Seuss" for his regular *Judge* feature called "'Boids and Beasties." This animal-based cartoon mixed fact and fiction, but usually was heavily weighted toward the fiction side—and Geisel's silliness. He thought adding the formal "Dr." to his name made the signature look more professional. He quipped that he saved his father a lot of money by becoming a doctor without going to medical school.

Geisel accidentally discovered that interesting things could happen if he used the name of a real product in one of his cartoons. A soda-water bottling company sent him four-dozen bottles of soda water after he used the brand name in a cartoon. In the summer of 1928, Geisel had an idea for a cartoon about the peskiness of bugs. In those days, people used a spray gun filled with insecticide to keep mosquitoes, flies, and other pests away during the heat of summer. Geisel drew a picture of a dragon flying above a knight. According to Morgan, the knight was saying, "Darn it all, another Dragon. And just after I'd sprayed the whole castle with Flit!" At the time, Geisel flipped a coin to decide whether to use the brand name "Flit" (made by the Standard Oil Company) or its competitor "Fly-Tox." As Geisel's never-ending luck had it, "Flit" won.

The wife of an advertising executive for Flit saw the ad while getting her hair done one day. She showed it to her husband and he contacted Geisel right away. That single cartoon (helped by the flip of a coin) landed Geisel a 17-year relationship as the cartoonist for Flit. One of Geisel's phrases was used over and over, though his drawings changed. Each time the cartoon read: "Quick, Henry, the Flit!" The advertisements appeared in magazines, on billboards, in newspapers, and even in the subway. In 1929, a collection of the ads was published as a booklet. This was Geisel's first exclusive publication—in a way, his first "book." All told, he published more than 125 Flit cartoons.

Sales of Flit increased dramatically. From that account alone, Geisel earned $12,000 a year, a large income at the time. Everyone loved those ads, though some people thought that his bugs were almost too lovable to spray with insecticide. Some other lovable creatures appeared in these ads, too—including one that clearly became the kind-hearted elephant, Horton.

Ted Geisel works on illustrations for one of his children's books at his desk at home in La Jolla, California, in April 1957. Unlike other children's authors, Dr. Seuss would lay out his own pages instead of letting his publishing company's editors and designers dictate the look of his books.

4

First Children's Books

THE 1920s WERE A TIME of wealth and prosperity for the country, but the last year of the decade brought financial trouble. On October 28, 1929, known as "Black Friday," the stock market crashed. Ted Geisel heard about it on the radio. In the 1920s, people had invested a lot of money in the stock market because the price of each share of stock generally kept rising. For example, RCA (Radio Corporation of America) had an all-time high of $505 per share on September 3, 1929. After the stock market crash, however, RCA stock tumbled to $28 per share. The Great Depression had begun, and it would last through the 1930s, ending only with America's entrance into

World War II. Ted and Helen Geisel did not suffer the same losses that many other Americans did. Still, Ted worried about the homeless, jobless Americans and was upset that he could do nothing to help. According to Morgan, Ted was deeply affected by "all these people who have nowhere to go." Geisel's father continued to work as superintendent of the park. Tragically, however, his mother, Henrietta Geisel, died in March 1931. It was one of the saddest days in Ted's life.

Geisel kept busy over the next several years. He drew and sold more advertisements. His first book opportunity came in 1931 when an editor at Viking Press asked him to illustrate a book of children's funny sayings. The funny words came from children's school papers in England. In the United States, the book was titled *Boners*, from a word that means "a funny mistake." (It was called *Schoolboy Howlers* in England.) It sold so well that a sequel, *More Boners*, was published later the same year.

Because Geisel's illustrations received positive reviews, he decided he wanted to write and illustrate his own children's book, an ABC book filled with strange animals. No one, however, was interested in his outlandish, bright-colored book. He put it aside when he and Helen became preoccupied moving into a nicer home on Park Avenue, where Ted set up a studio. "His desk had lots of charcoal, pencils, and paint brushes," said Helen's niece Barbara Palmer, as quoted by Morgan. After a while, Ted and Helen began to travel extensively. He always took a sketchpad with him when he traveled. Once it was filled, he used hotel stationery. But his love of children's books was not gone for good. Soon his off-the-wall ideas ignited his imagination again.

FROM BUG SPRAY TO CHILDREN'S BOOKS

At a time when many Americans had to pinch their pennies, Ted and Helen Geisel were able to travel to Europe, Latin America, and the Middle East. Besides making a good income from his advertisements, Geisel also was commissioned privately to create some paintings and murals for some well-to-do people. One of the most famous was done at the Lexington, Kentucky, home of the Edwards family, which is now the Kentucky Horse Park. His success gave him the money and time to be able to take much-needed vacations. In some ways, these trips were more than vacations for him; he needed the stimulation of new places and new people in order to keep his creativity going. Never was this truer than on the MS *Kungsholm*, bound for Europe in the summer of 1936. The Geisels' time there (and especially their storm-ridden trip home) was just the right experience at just the right time for Geisel to launch his children's book career with *And to Think That I Saw It on Mulberry Street!*

Within a few months, *And to Think That I Saw It on Mulberry Street!* was on its way to becoming the kind of book that would delight children and adults alike. Few authors have the immediate welcome that "Dr. Seuss" had. Reviewers loved the new style of his writing, not to mention the zany drawings that made the stories especially unusual. Vanguard Press, the book's publisher, ordered 15,000 copies to be printed, a large amount even for today. Two years later, a second printing of 6,000 copies was made. Still, it did not look as if Geisel was going to get rich by writing and illustrating children's books. An author often is paid a royalty—a percentage of the sales of his or her book. In 1937, Dr. Seuss's *Mulberry Street* sold for one dollar. Even if he earned 10 percent as a royalty (a typical percentage for a royalty), he would earn only 10 cents for each book sold. In that case, the first print run would have earned the good Dr. Seuss only $1,500. In fact, by 1943, he had earned only $3,500 from *Mulberry Street*.

Not that Geisel was worried about money. He was still making a very good living by writing and drawing ads, mostly for the giant Standard Oil Company. Creating children's books was just one more way for Dr. Seuss to express the sights and sounds alive within his active mind. Helen, who knew him best, understood that he was captivated by the fun of creating children's books. In fact, according to Morgan, Helen once said, "His mind has never grown up."

Geisel's childhood love of costumes never grew up either. One day, while visiting Ted and Helen, his sister Marnie found that her brother had collected hundreds of hats, including some very old and very weird ones. He told her that he liked to use them to entertain his friends when they came over for dinner. He had firemen's hats, old helmets, admirals' hats—anything big and heavily decorated. These hats became important as he started his next book, *The 500 Hats of Bartholomew Cubbins*. Unlike *Mulberry Street*, this book did not use lines that rhymed. Instead, it was written in prose as a fairy tale. Also different from the multicolored illustrations in *Mulberry Street*, the art in *The 500 Hats* was black and white, except for Bartholomew's hat, which was bright red.

Geisel got his idea for the book while riding the train from Springfield to New York one day. A gentleman in front of him caught Geisel's attention. According to Weidt, Geisel recalled, "He had a real ridiculous Wall Street broker's hat on—very stuffy. And I just began playing around with the idea of what his reaction would be if I took his hat off and threw it out the window. I decided that he was so stuffy that he'd probably grow another one." So Bartholomew Cubbins ended up with the same problem: hats that kept growing from his head. When Geisel started writing the story, Bartholomew had only 48 hats, then he gave him 135, and eventually was satisfied when he had made the number an even 500. *The 500 Hats* came out in 1938.

Did you know...

In the prosperous 1920s, so many children's books were produced that it became the fastest-growing part of the whole publishing industry. The Great Depression forced publishers to cut back on how many books they could publish, especially on the number of expensive-to-produce colorful picture books. Sometimes cutting back can be a good thing, though. In this case, it meant that publishers would spend their money to produce fewer but better books. Despite the hard times, some of the best-loved picture books of the twentieth century were published in the 1930s, including *The Little Engine That Could, The Story of Babar, The Story about Ping,* and *The Story of Ferdinand.*

Picture-book collectors find that some first-edition copies of these books, as well as three of Dr. Seuss's—*And to Think That I Saw It on Mulberry Street!, The 500 Hats of Bartholomew Cubbins,* and *The King's Stilts—* are worth hundreds or even thousands of dollars.

Authors and illustrators normally turn their work over to the editors and designers in the publishing company so these experts can prepare the book for print. Editors and designers typically work with the words, the art, the colors, and the design to create what they think will be the best book possible. Rather than turning his books over to the publisher and waiting for his books to appear in print, Geisel liked to be involved in every step of the process. His eye for color and composition (how a page looks when everything is in place) was nearly perfect. In fact, he often made his own dummies (samples of the finished product) by cutting and pasting the words and pictures on each page until they were just right. In those days, this meant *really* cutting and pasting—using scissors and glue to put pages together. Some of these dummies of his books still exist in museums.

The reviews of Dr. Seuss's *The 500 Hats* were even stronger than the ones he had received for *Mulberry Street*. According to the Morgan biography, one reviewer stated it was "a complete tale, not too long, not too short, just right." Of all the reviews he would read during his life, Ted's favorite was written about this book. An old college friend wrote: "I do not see what is to prevent him from becoming the Grimm of our times." The name "Dr. Seuss" was unusual enough to be easy to remember—if you knew how to say it. Up to this time, Ted had pronounced "Seuss" in the traditional way, "*soice*," but he found that people remembered it better if it were pronounced differently. He let them "mispronounce" *Seuss* so it rhymed with Mother *Goose*. Of course, that made sense to everyone! And it has been pronounced this way ever since.

Ted and Helen had been married for 11 years when *The 500 Hats* hit the bookstore shelves. They decided to

Ted Geisel shows his wife, Helen, sketches for his book, How the Grinch Stole Christmas!, *on their patio in front of their house in La Jolla, California, on April 25, 1957. Helen would edit many of her husband's books.*

dedicate this book to their imaginary child, "Chrysanthemum Pearl, age 89 months, going on 90." The Geisels even added her name (and a few others, including Norval, Thnud, and Wickersham) as they signed their Christmas cards. Helen was unable to have children, but that did not keep her and her husband from enjoying their nieces and nephews or the children who came to have their books autographed. When adults asked him why he had no children of his own, Geisel usually replied, according to Weidt, "You have 'em, I'll amuse 'em."

A MAN IN DEMAND

Geisel was as successful a beginning author as Vanguard Press had ever had. It came as no surprise, then, when a powerhouse publisher tried to get Geisel to write books for him instead. Bennett Cerf, publisher of Random House, was well known in the book business. The two men met for lunch one day, and they liked each other immediately. By the time lunch was over, Geisel had agreed to write his next book for Random House. At first Geisel felt guilty about leaving the publishing company that had given him his first chance, but Vanguard was a small house and was unable to devote as much time and money to promote his books as he liked. He knew that Random House could do a better job of marketing his books.

Despite the marketing, Geisel's first book with Random House was also his first failure as an author. *The Seven Lady Godivas* (1939) was not a children's book. That may have been his first mistake. Adults were not ready (or apparently interested) in buying a book with silly pictures of women and even sillier words about them. Bennett Cerf and Geisel knew he was best at writing for children, so they agreed that his next book would bring "the good Dr. Seuss" back to younger readers. His contract with Random House was revised, setting his royalty rates for children's books at 10 percent for the first 5,000 copies sold and 15 percent for each copy above 5,000. This was a very good deal.

Helen became her husband's best editor, not only on this book, but also on the many more that followed. They worked well together, making sure the words were just right. "Her words are in some of them," Geisel said, according to Morgan. Ted worked alone on the illustrations. He started by making pencil sketches side by side, just as they would appear on facing pages. It usually took him several months before a book was ready to take to his editor. In 1939, Random House published his first children's book with them—*The King's Stilts*, which brought back Bartholomew Cubbins. This was another fairy tale with Dr. Seuss's strange, but wonderful touch. The author surprised Helen's nieces when he stilt-walked up the front steps of their house on Thanksgiving Day, continued walking inside the house, and then worked his way around the dining room table. He told them that he had learned how to walk on stilts when he was doing research for his book.

Geisel's next Random House book was born from some doodles. He often sketched random pictures in pencil on tracing paper while trying to think of ideas for new stories. On New Year's Day of 1940, he looked down at a familiar face. The sweet expression that looked back at him belonged to an elephant that seemed related to the blue one he had drawn in *Mulberry Street*. After he returned from his desk from getting a cup of coffee in the kitchen, he found that the wind from an open window had blown some of his papers around a bit. Tracing paper is nearly transparent, so something interesting happened when one piece landed on top of another. One paper had the elephant sketch on it;

the other had a tree. After the wind did its job, the elephant suddenly looked as if he were sitting high up in a tree. Now *that* was a story! Tree. Elephant. Sitting. Nest. Egg. From this "accidental" event came the next book: *Horton Hatches the Egg.* This was the only book he ever wrote for which he could explain how he had come up with the idea. "I've left a window open by my desk ever since," he once said, according to Morgan, "but it never happened again."

He worked hard on this book, as usual, and found he had trouble with two things: what to name the characters and how to get the elephant out of the tree. The main character had many names, such as Osmer, Bosco, and Humphrey, but eventually was named Horton after one of Geisel's college friends. The bird was named Bessie, then Saidie, and finally Mayzie. According to the Morgan biography, the author was delighted with how the book was going:

> The new book is coming along with a rapidity that leaves me breathless. It is a beautiful thing. The funniest juvenile [book] ever written. I mean, being written. Never before have I stood before myself and pointed so proudly, saying, "Genius, you are." I feel certain it will sell well over a million. . . . P.S.: I like my new book.

Geisel turned to Helen to help him get Horton back to Earth, however. In fact, it was she who wrote the solution: "It's something brand new! IT'S AN ELEPHANT-BIRD!!"

In June 1940, as Geisel was in the middle of work on the book, a frightening event took place in Europe—Hitler's Nazi troops had invaded and defeated France. (France and Great Britain had been at war with Germany since the German invasion of Poland, which took place on September 1, 1939.) In America, images of a kindhearted elephant were pushed aside as Ted began angrily sketching an evil Adolf

Hitler instead. As Britain fought alone against the Axis powers of Germany, Italy, and Japan throughout the fall of 1940, the United States had remained neutral militarily (not on one side or another), but had aided the Allies financially. No American soldiers were involved—yet.

When *Horton Hatches the Egg* arrived in bookstores that autumn, it was a remarkable success right away. This book settled any questions the 36-year-old Geisel had about what he was going to do with his life. As usual, reviewers adored the Dr. Seuss book. The famous New York toy store, FAO Schwarz, created a big window display featuring an elephant sitting in a tree. Geisel enjoyed seeing how people loved his work and accepted many invitations at bookstores to do author signings of his books, both for children and adults. He never took his readers lightly, knowing it was his job to entertain them with words and pictures.

Even so, as America's involvement in World War II seemed likely, Ted knew that deadly serious things were happening that he cared about, too. He began drawing political cartoons about the Nazis and Fascists in Europe. Some of these were published in the winter of 1941 in a New York periodical named *PM*. The editor asked him to draw more. For the next seven years, Geisel turned away from the fantasy world of children's literature to help his country as they faced some very real enemies: the Axis powers.

Ted Geisel reclines with his Irish setter Cluny and some proofs of his work by the edge of his swimming pool in La Jolla, California. After World War II, the Geisels moved to California because they had fallen in love with the sunny climate.

Netherlands, Greece, and Yugoslavia and their bombings of England came through loud and clear. Just as disturbing was the news that the Japanese were becoming hostile, too. Few Americans were convinced that the United States would be in a war with Japan, but Geisel saw it coming.

THE ART AND ANIMATION OF WAR

Dr. Seuss put aside his children's books for the next seven years as Ted Geisel turned his talents toward helping our country during a difficult time. Adolf Hitler, who was making his father's homeland an enemy of America, especially upset the author. When doing political cartoons for *PM* during the war years, he often drew Hitler as a demanding baby in diapers. Later he admitted that these cartoons were not his best artwork, because they had to be put together so quickly; he often had to draw as many as five per week. Geisel drew political cartoons for the magazine for two years, from early 1941 to the beginning of 1943.

The Geisels returned to New York in November. Only one month later, on December 7, 1941, they heard the now-famous radio announcement that the Japanese had bombed the U.S. Navy base at Pearl Harbor in Hawaii. Geisel's reaction was immediate: He ran to his drawing board and began drawing furiously. One of his cartoons showed a cat-like Uncle Sam that had been awakened from sleep to find himself at war. On December 8, the U.S. Congress declared war on Japan; three days later, Germany and Italy, Japan's allies, declared war on the United States, and the U.S. government responded in kind.

Suddenly, the United States was at war both in Asia against Japan and in Europe against Hitler's Germany. Geisel's cartoons drew a lot of attention, both good and bad. Isolationists—people who wanted America to stay out

5

Dr. Seuss
Goes to War

IN JUNE 1941, TED AND HELEN Geisel left New York to spend the summer at a house they had recently purchased for $8,000 (partially with his royalty advance for *Horton Hatches an Egg*) in La Jolla, California. According to Judith and Neil Morgan's book, *Dr. Seuss and Mr. Geisel*, the happy, sun-struck author loved California and wrote to his editor in New York, telling her that he had to "fight rattlesnakes, bees, and man-eating rabbits in the patio." Both he and Helen felt at home in this town near San Diego. Even there, however, the news from Europe of the Nazi invasions of Poland, Czechoslovakia, Denmark, Norway, France, Belgium, Luxembourg, the

Did you know...

Between 1939 and 1941, the United States watched as Germany and Japan invaded nearby countries, bombing cities and killing people. The war was "over there"—in Europe and in Asia. Most Americans still remembered the pains of World War I and many did not want to get involved in another war that would send American soldiers so far away. People who held that opinion were known as isolationists, meaning they preferred to remain isolated from the fighting. One of the most outspoken isolationists was Charles A. Lindbergh, the famous pilot who in 1927 became the first person to fly across the Atlantic Ocean. His fame continued when his firstborn son was kidnapped and murdered in 1932. Because the media would not leave them alone, Charles and his wife, Anne Morrow Lindbergh, moved to Europe to gain privacy.

Lindbergh watched as the Nazi regime under Adolf Hitler revived the broken economy of Germany. He visited Germany twice, in 1936 and 1937, and was "impressed" with the German military and with its people. He and his wife even considered moving there in 1938, the same year he was given Germany's Service Cross on Hitler's behalf. A month later, the Nazis destroyed Jewish businesses in an event now known as *Kristallnacht*. The Lindberghs decided to return to America in 1939, where he asserted that he believed no one could defeat the Nazis in a war. Because of this position and some anti-Semitic (anti-Jewish) statements, Lindbergh would never be seen in the same light again.

of the war—did not like his cartoons, especially the ones that ridiculed the American hero and isolationist, Charles Lindbergh. (Lindbergh was Geisel's second-most-frequent subject; Hitler was his first.) Some of his cartoons featured people wearing "ostrich bonnets" given to them by the "Lindy Ostrich Service"—since ostriches are known for sticking their heads in the sand, ignoring what is going on around them.

But others loved Geisel's political cartoons. According to Morgan, *Newsweek* said his editorial cartoons were "razor-keen." The Treasury Department and the War Production Board also liked his work and commissioned him to create posters to help the war effort. By the summer of 1942, Ted and Helen Geisel had returned to California, where Ted kept busy with posters and cartoons. Living on the West Coast during the war was a strange time. Threats and rumors of Japanese invasions of San Diego made it necessary for the military to practice maneuvers in case such an attack really would take place. With an ocean view from their La Jolla home, the Geisels often saw dive-bombing airplanes, numerous boats, and even some tanks.

Frustrated that he was not able to do more to help the war cause, Geisel, though well past the draft age, signed up for the U.S. Navy, requesting to work in naval intelligence. Before he could be accepted, he was offered a commission with the U.S. Army, where he was stationed with the Signal Corps, which was then headed by award-winning movie director Frank Capra, in Hollywood, California. Head-quartered at a Twentieth-Century Fox studio near Sunset Boulevard, this unit was responsible for creating film footage for the troops. Some of the nation's best animators and illustrators were there as well. P.D. Eastman, who later illustrated some of Dr. Seuss's Beginner Books, met Ted at

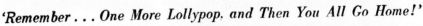

'Remember . . . One More Lollypop, and Then You All Go Home!'

During World War II, Ted Geisel used his talents as an illustrator for the war effort. This cartoon by Dr. Seuss, drawn for the progressive New York daily PM *in the early 1940s, is one of 200 political cartoons by the artist featured in the 1999 book* Dr. Seuss Goes to War.

"Fort Fox," as they called the place. Well-known animation artists Friz Freleng and Chuck Jones, who had worked at Warner Brothers, were among the talented men of the unit. During his time in the Signal Corps, Theodor Geisel wore a uniform and practiced drills, just as any soldier would, but his weapons against the enemy were words and pictures, not guns.

Helen moved to Hollywood to be with her husband and kept busy with her own writing while he was at Fox Studios.

She wrote prose books for Disney and Golden Books, leaving the rhyming to Dr. Seuss. In all her attempts to write children's books, only one was rejected. Some of her better-known books include *Three Caballeros*, *Donald Duck Sees South America*, and *Walt Disney's Surprise Package*. Later Geisel said that she supported them financially during the war. She and her husband did not like Los Angeles as much as they enjoyed La Jolla. The city was big, was packed with commuters on the highways, and was starting to be covered by a strange smoke-like fog that became known as "smog."

The Fort Fox unit put together newsreels for soldiers to see. They created a new one every two weeks. Part of the newsreel, which kept the troops informed of news about the war and the homeland, included cartoons. These cartoons usually had to do with some element of training that the men needed to learn. At first, the film troop used real actors for these pieces, but they soon found that the soldiers responded much better to animated pieces. Here is where Geisel learned about animated cartoons, something that would be important later in his career. He and Chuck Jones became especially good friends.

Geisel's greatest work during the war, however, was not a cartoon. After being promoted to major, he began work on a special project, *Your Job in Germany*, a film for soldiers who would move into Germany at the end of the war, free the country, and bring it back to health. But first, the film had to be reviewed and accepted by the American generals in the newly liberated city of Aachen, Germany. This meant Geisel had to go there in person to show them the film. He heard bombs overhead and the loud thuds of artillery hitting their mark. After the screening, he was moved to Bastogne, France, because military intelligence had

It's a Cinch, Adolf...Once You Learn to Play It

During World War II, Geisel drew hundreds of political cartoons, like this one for many periodicals. Geisel also branched out into film and helped create newsreels and orientation movies for the military.

cleared it as a quiet, safer place. Within hours, the Battle of the Bulge—a major German offensive launched toward the end of the war—began, leaving Geisel on the wrong side of the front. "We learned we were ten miles [16 kilometers] behind German lines. We were trapped three days before being rescued by the British," he later explained, according to Morgan. Once his mission was finished, and the generals approved of his film, Ted returned to California. It was January 1945. Only three months later, Germany would fall to the Allied forces, and his film was ready to show soldiers what to do when they occupied a fallen Germany. After the film was shown, filmmaker Don Siegel used it as the basis for his documentary, *Hitler Lives*, and it won an Academy Award in 1946.

World War II ended when the Japanese surrendered in August 1945. The Geisels' celebration of peace, however, did not last long. On September 14, 1945, Ted's dear sister, Marnie, died of a heart attack. She was only 43 years old. Her death was one of the few things that he could never talk about. He missed her terribly. Ted and Helen became like parents to Marnie's daughter Peggy, who loved her uncle and aunt and knew they would always be available if she needed them.

After the war, Geisel tried to work on more films in Hollywood for a while. He and Helen were asked to work together to create a documentary about Japan that was based on a film Geisel wrote in the army, *Our Job in Japan*. This was a very frustrating experience for him, since Geisel was used to having more control over the things he made. In the end, after 32 revisions, *Design for Death* was shown and gathered strong reviews. In 1947, it won the Academy Award for best documentary feature. Ted and Helen were at the ceremony when the award was announced. Two years later, the film mysteriously disappeared and has not been seen since.

Helen wondered if Dr. Seuss would return to write children's books. A lot had happened in seven years, and being silly and childlike was not as easy as it once had been.

BACK TO THE BOOKS

After the war, for those who had survived the Great Depression and World War II, family life became more important than ever before. In the late 1940s and the 1950s, new suburbs emerged as families built homes in communities away from the bustle of the city. During this time, referred to as the baby boom, children were born in record numbers—very good news to the children's book business. Now that people had money to spend, they liked to spend it on their children. The timing was perfect for Dr. Seuss to reappear.

By 1946, Geisel, unsatisfied working as a filmmaker, knew it was time to renew his relationship with the publishing world—and with Bennett Cerf at Random House in particular. Geisel was pleased to find that many new improvements had come along to make book printing even more visually appealing. These new printing methods allowed many more colors and much richer hues to be used on the page. Nothing could have made Dr. Seuss happier. In short order, the author made two decisions: first, to return to his work as a children's book writer and illustrator, and second, to move to sunny California permanently after spending the summer of 1946 living at some friends' villa near Los Angeles. According to Thomas Fensch's book *The Man Who Was Dr. Seuss*, he said that he liked the idea of being able "to walk around outside in my pajamas."

The warm climate was the perfect place for Geisel to begin his next book, *McElligot's Pool*, published in 1947. Marco reappeared as a main character, fishing in a pool where he imagines the strangest aquatic creatures ever: a half-cow fish, a kangaroo-like fish, and a dogfish. Experts praised the illustrations as Seuss's best ever. The watercolors he chose for this book were rich and beautiful; it was the only book he ever did in watercolor, mainly because, according to Morgan, he had a "mortal fear" that his books might look "like a comic book." The watercolors fit the water-world he had created. Few people were surprised when *McElligot's Pool* won a Caldecott Honor award. The Caldecott Medal winner and Caldecott Honor books are chosen as the best-illustrated books each year. Seuss's book also became a Junior Literary Guild selection, a distinction that set it apart from other picture books.

The next Seuss book appeared in 1948. Simply colored in only red, black, and blue, *Thidwick the Big-Hearted Moose* greeted both children and adults and became Geisel's second Junior Literary Guild selection. Thidwick is a gentle moose who lets others take advantage of his goodness. In the end, however, the freeloaders get what is coming to them, while Thidwick remains just as bighearted as ever. Along with the publication of this book, this was also the year that Ted and Helen moved permanently to La Jolla, California, to a place they called "The Tower" because it actually was a tower on Mount Soledad, high above the rest of the town. Ted and Helen made this their home for the rest of their lives.

Geisel was on a literary roll and, for a while, continued to create a book a year. He loved his new workroom, which overlooked the Pacific Ocean and the beautiful southern California coastline. But when it was time to work, he turned his back to the beauty so it would not distract him. He set himself an eight-hour schedule, seven days a week. Sometimes he worked much longer, late into the night, taking only short breaks. He still used the same wooden drawing board that he had started with in New York during the 1930s. All around were containers holding colored pencils, stained paintbrushes, and stubs of erasers. He seldom threw away anything on his desk, including one-inch-long (2.5-centimeter-long) pencils that had been used as much as they could be.

Typically, Geisel sat in a high-backed chair, and he swiveled back and forth as he thought. First, he sketched his illustrations on tracing paper; then he drew the pictures and wrote the words for one page, perfecting each page before starting on the next. This often took draft after draft before he was ready to draw his final illustration on heavy paper with a felt-tip pen. According to Weidt, his pile of throwaway drafts was called "the bone pile." If he got stuck in his writing, he often paced back and forth across the room, or, if he was really "blocked," he would pick out one of his many hats and wear it until an idea came to him. "It's hard," he once said, according to Fensch's biography. "I'm a bleeder and I sweat at it. . . . You have to remember that in a children's book a paragraph is like a chapter in an adult book, and a sentence is like a paragraph." Other times, he reclined on a couch in his workroom and read a mystery novel until he was a little tired. According to Morgan, he said his "best stuff" was written when he was "a bit tired."

Some of his ideas came more easily than others, though. Resurrecting Marco had been a good idea in *McElligot's*

Pool, Ted figured, so why not bring back Bartholomew Cubbins, the boy with 500 hats? In 1949, *Bartholomew and the Oobleck* gave children the goo of their dreams: gloppy green goo called "oobleck" that rains over everything in the kingdom. "I didn't dream it up," Ted explained about the idea, according to Morgan. While in Europe during World War II, he overheard a soggy soldier complain, "Rain, always rain! Why can't we have something different for a change?" That was all he needed to get his creative wheels turning. In the story, the King gets his magicians to change the rain, snow, and fog to oobleck. Disaster results when the goo smothers everything. Then, like verbal magic, the goo stops falling only after the great king admits, "It's all my fault." Geisel won his second Caldecott Honor Award for this gooey tale, which has only two colors: black and (of course) green.

BITS OF WRITING WISDOM

Geisel overcame his stage fright temporarily when he was asked to speak at a writer's conference in 1949. The trick he used when the fear started to rise up inside him was to find a chalkboard and sketch illustrations all over it. According to Morgan, his panic nearly returned this time when he discovered all of his drawings had been erased by a janitor who thought that "some kids really messed up the blackboard." He pushed through, however, and offered some simple advice to the would-be authors who came to learn from him. "Write a verse a day," he told them, as quoted by Morgan, "not to send to publishers, but to throw in waste baskets. It will help your prose. . . . Shorten paragraphs and sentences, then shorten words. . . . Use verbs. Let the kids fill in the adjectives."

After the conference, Geisel wanted to start working on a book about children's book writing. His editor did not feel as strongly about the project as Geisel. He preferred that Dr. Seuss return to writing his own books rather than telling others how to do it. Although quite disappointed, Geisel began work on his next project, *If I Ran the Zoo*.

While settling into his new home in California, Geisel often thought back about his childhood in Springfield on Fairfield Street. Some of the most vivid memories included the sights, sounds, smells, and impressions of the Springfield Zoo, where he, his father, and his sister had spent time exploring the animal kingdom. More and more, his thoughts ran wild—all about the zoo. Staring out his window, Geisel began an imaginative journey that would become one of his funniest, warmest books ever. *If I Ran the Zoo* appeared in 1950 to glowing reviews and eventually earned another Caldecott Honor Award. A new decade was underway, and Dr. Seuss was just getting warmed up.

Dr. Seuss (Theodor Seuss Geisel) sits at his drafting table in his home office with a copy of his most famous book, **The Cat in the Hat,** *shortly after its publication in 1957.*

6

New Dreams—and One Bad Nightmare

WITH EIGHT SUCCESSFUL children's books already claiming space in bookstores all across the country, Ted Geisel still found himself thinking about making films in Hollywood. He stayed in touch with some of his World War II buddies who continued to work there. One in particular, P.D. Eastman, was an illustrator with the new United Productions of America studio. While most studios were using the same kinds of storylines in their cartoons, UPA wanted to try something different. Eastman knew that Geisel was just the person to approach. No one had proven to have fresher ideas than Dr. Seuss. And, as usual, the good doctor did not disappoint his friend or his fans.

Dr. Seuss's first full-length children's cartoon started from one big idea: "Just suppose," he suggested, according to Morgan, "there was a little kid who didn't speak words but only weird sounds." Because he felt he was not good at drawing people, he wanted someone else to do the illustrations for the cartoon. *Gerald McBoing Boing* was about a "different" kid who is teased and pushed aside because he makes strange noises, like a horse's neigh or a squeaky door. After running away, Gerald is "discovered" by a man who wants the boy to make his noises as special effects on the radio. His talent is finally recognized, and Gerald is a big success. So were Geisel and UPA Studios. In 1950, *Gerald McBoing Boing* won an Academy Award for best cartoon. At the same time, copies of *If I Ran the Zoo* were selling as fast as they hit the shelves.

DR. SEUSS'S FANTASY FILM

Helen Geisel had worked tirelessly with her husband as his editor and critic—and as his assistant in answering his mail and phone calls. In responding to some of the fan letters, she even signed herself "Mrs. Dr. Seuss." But the pace was difficult for Helen, and her health was affected. Though tired and suffering from painful ulcers, she kept working, happy for his success. Things were just beginning to get even busier.

The thrill of working with film was alive in Geisel again. He sent an idea for another feature-length film to Columbia Studios. The three-time Academy Award winner was offered a $35,000 advance for his newest idea, a fantasy film called *The 5,000 Fingers of Dr. T.* This time, he planned to include real children in the movie alongside animated characters. The plot centered around one boy who hated taking piano lessons and his rescue of hundreds of other children who were enslaved to their pianos by the evil Dr. Terwilliger. Happy beyond description, Geisel expected to become immersed in the film process and to have control over "his" project. Helen, however, was concerned that this might be one of the busiest years of their lives—and a year without a new book. She knew that this was one of her husband's greatest dreams, so she was willing to sacrifice whatever was needed to make him happy. In fact, the Geisels rented an apartment in Los Angeles so he could easily get to the studio each weekday. On the weekends, the Geisels returned to La Jolla.

What began as a grand idea and thrilling experience quickly dissolved into trouble. Geisel wrote the screenplay and the lyrics to the songs, but someone was constantly changing things. The changes continued to happen, causing the production of the film to be postponed three times. At least his set designs stayed true to his style. At one point, Geisel told the producer that he was leaving the film because the script changes were more than he could tolerate. Some compromising took place, and he stayed on.

A year after beginning the project, the cast was finally ready for filming, just as significant budget cuts were announced. One way to make cuts was to use fewer actors; where the script had called for 500 boy pianists (from which the title *5,000 Fingers* comes), only 150 were really used. But there were good times on the set as well. One day, someone made the mistake of paying each of the boys his weekly pay rather than giving it to the child's parent or agent. After a hotdog-eating spree at the lunchroom, one of the boys threw up all over his piano. "This started a chain reaction, causing one after another of the boys to go queasy in the greatest mass upchuck in the history of Hollywood," said Geisel, as quoted by Morgan. "When the picture was finally released, the critics reacted in much the same manner." When the film was previewed, most of the audience left the theater after only 15 minutes. For the rest of his life, Ted described making this film as, according to Weidt, "the worst experience of my life." He refused even to list it in his biography at Random House.

BACK HOME IN LA JOLLA

After the filming was finished, Geisel hurried back to his home office in La Jolla to finish his next book for Random House, one that had been due in January. In May, he was still at work on *Scrambled Eggs Super!* He had missed the chance to have it available to bookstores by Christmas, so it came out in March 1953, just before he and Helen sailed for Japan. The editors of *Life* had asked him to write a piece for them about the children of Japan. On board, the Geisels studied information about how Japan had changed since World War II. His job was to find out how the war had changed the hopes and plans of the children there.

Geisel crossed the language barrier by having the children do what he best understood: illustrating. He asked them to draw pictures of what they wanted to be when they grew up. In all, he collected more than 15,000 drawings. Not surprisingly, the drawings often reflected a more modern kind of thinking—and a more Americanized thinking, too. Boys saw themselves being pilots; girls wanted to be hostesses, much like flight attendants. Geisel adored the children and the work he accomplished in Japan, but was once again disappointed with the end product when the editors of *Life* changed his article to reflect their own ideas instead of Ted's. Even so, his and Helen's adventures in Japan helped soothe the irritation of the *5,000 Fingers* fiasco. He was determined to let go of the film world and to fully embrace his greatest gift: writing and illustrating children's books. He had only one question: Could he make

Did you know...

After Japan surrendered and World War II ended, the United States began an occupation of Japan. President Harry Truman sent General Douglas MacArthur to Japan as supreme commander of the occupation forces. The main focus of the occupation was to reform the political and economic structures of Japan. All of the war leaders were removed from power. The Japanese government wrote and adopted a new constitution, making Japan a democracy. The emperor was no longer the sovereign leader of Japan, but remained a symbolic leader, similar to the British monarch. Political power now belonged to the people. The new constitution guaranteed citizens the right to free speech. Women were given the right to vote. The military was abolished, with the promise that Japan would never again build an army or go to war.

The United States sent a tremendous amount of money and supplies to Japan to help rebuild their country. Schools began to teach children the concepts and values of democracy. Most Japanese were open to the changes brought about by the U.S. occupation because they were upset with their own leaders during the war. Long after U.S. troops have left Japan, the Japanese have continued to maintain an effective democracy and have built a strong economy.

Ted Geisel holds a bust of one of his characters, a blue-green abelard, in his workroom in La Jolla, California. Creating strange and fantastical creatures had been one of his themes since the start of his cartooning career.

a real living doing only that? At this point, he was earning only a few hundred dollars a year from his books' royalties. Most of his other work, mainly in advertising and filmmaking, had kept him financially secure. As it turned out, the baby boom would make it possible for Dr. Seuss to earn more than enough.

As citizens of La Jolla, the Geisels joined some civic groups so they could get involved in the community. They made many friends and loved to socialize. Ted was especially fond of playing practical jokes, as always, and Helen often had to talk him out of his most ridiculous ideas. When things were not going well with his writing, he would walk around his property, looking at the plants and moving rocks here and there, arranging them in ways that pleased him. His best-loved "rock" was carefully placed in a shaded garden. Many years previously, his father had given him a rock that held a true dinosaur's footprint. Over the years, Ted had taken that rock with him whenever he moved. Finally, it found a permanent home.

In late 1953, Geisel started a new book that brought back his beloved character, Horton the elephant. Writing in verse again (this one actually has the same rhythm as "'Twas the Night Before Christmas"), Ted used his experience in Japan to develop a wonderful theme: "A person's a person no matter how small." *Horton Hears a Who!* was very much a Ted-and-Helen joint effort. She helped him maintain his rhythm while not losing sight of the message. In early 1954, the Geisels went to New York to hand-deliver the manuscript and illustrations. The editors and publisher gathered in one office as the author read the story out loud. There was no doubt that another Seuss bestseller had just been born.

Traveling, writing, speaking, and entertaining kept Ted and Helen Geisel under pressure throughout 1954. This year brought many challenges and one great honor. Geisel was called to receive an honorary doctorate degree from his college, Dartmouth. The Geisels were excited, but decided to keep the news to themselves for a while. During a party to celebrate the new concert season in La Jolla, someone mentioned a new article in *Life*. The article suggested Dr. Seuss might be a good author/illustrator to take on the job of making reading fun for school children. Most schools were then using the monotonous "Dick and Jane" books for reading instruction. He might have become immersed in this project right away if Helen's health had not suddenly taken a turn for the worse. Within 24 hours of the party, Helen was in great pain and quickly became paralyzed from the neck down.

Doctors at first were puzzled by her symptoms, but they diagnosed her with Guillain-Barré syndrome, a typically fatal disease. Because Helen could not breathe on her own, she was placed in a machine called an iron lung, which would breathe for her. This is a large metal machine in which a patient's entire body is placed. Only her head stuck out, and a mirror was placed above her so she could see around her. The doctors told Geisel that her chance of surviving was very small.

Helen's condition worsened over the next two weeks to the point that she did not recognize her husband any longer. Geisel stayed near her, and at night he helped the nurses by carrying things for them. He called Dartmouth College to tell them he would not be able to attend the ceremony to receive his degree. Each day that Helen survived was "a miracle," according to Morgan. His devotion to her was strong, and somehow Helen began to fight back. Soon she was able to breathe on her own and could swallow again.

He brought her Popsicles to help her practice swallowing. In July, she no longer needed the iron lung at all. Transferred to a rehabilitation hospital that month, Helen started her long journey back. Eventually she would regain the abilities to talk and walk again. She had to relearn the most basic things, such as buttoning her clothes or combing her hair. Geisel rented an apartment near the hospital so he could take care of the business and do some work. This was not easy for him, because Helen had always taken care of everything. He had not kept a checkbook or made coffee in decades. Somehow, he managed.

In August, Helen was well enough to enjoy her husband's happy news that *Horton Hears a Who!* was receiving positive reviews. In September, she was able to move back to La Jolla, but she could not be left alone. Despite the pain and difficulty, Helen worked hard at her physical therapy and made good progress. Through it all, Helen described Ted as "part man, part angel," according to Morgan. A very relieved and happy husband, Geisel had renewed energy to work on new projects, including his next book *On Beyond Zebra* (1955), which took children beyond the letter *Z* to such new ones as Yuzz and Vroo. He dedicated this book to Helen.

A few months later, in June 1956, Ted finally accepted his honorary doctorate degree from Dartmouth, making him "Dr. Dr. Seuss," as he liked to joke. Robert Frost, the great American poet, was also honored by Dartmouth that year. Ted said later, according to Morgan, "I very carefully refrained from mentioning [to him] the kind of poetry I write." The same year, his twelfth children's book was published. Modeled after the popular *If I Ran the Zoo*, he wrote *If I Ran the Circus* and dedicated it to his father. His next book, however, changed reading for children all over the country and would make Dr. Seuss perhaps the most recognized children's author in the United States.

Did you know...

In the 1950s, after many years of bad economic times and war worries, Americans finally had time and money to spend on things they enjoyed. Even so, the world was a different place, and it was changing more every day. Communism was a growing presence, as far away as the Soviet Union and as near as Cuba. The threat of nuclear attacks grew and the United States was competing with the Soviet Union in technology and space exploration. Americans were stunned when the Soviets moved ahead in the space race, launching the very first satellite, *Sputnik 1*, on October 4, 1957. Even more alarming was the launch of *Sputnik 2* only a month later, because this one was the first to send an animal—a dog named Laika—into space. The United States followed by launching its first satellite, *Explorer I*, on January 31, 1958, which then led to the creation of the National Aeronautics and Space Administration (NASA). This contest was about more than space exploration—it was about which world power could prove itself technologically superior. How could we compete when it seemed the Soviets were ahead of us in science and technology?

Some felt that answers lay in our educational system. Children's reading skills had to improve, and science and mathematics needed more emphasis. It was time for new approaches.

THE CAT IN THE HAT

Previously, in 1955, Geisel had traveled to Boston to meet with the head of publishing at Houghton Mifflin's education division. William Spaulding was concerned about the research that showed American children were becoming weaker readers. He felt that classroom teachers needed to have better reading books to share with their students, books with great illustrations as well as good stories. Dr. Seuss, Spaulding believed, was just the one to help out. During their meeting, he told Geisel, "Write me a story that first graders can't put down!" Then he handed the author a list of 225 words, challenging him to use only those words when he wrote the new book. Geisel was interested in the concept, but first had to complete work on *If I Ran the Circus*. Because of Geisel's contract with Random House, the publisher at Houghton Mifflin would have to get Bennett Cerf, his publisher, to agree. They agreed that Houghton Mifflin was allowed to sell a school edition to schools only, and Random House sold their trade edition in bookstores, as usual.

The limitations of a word list made writing more difficult than Geisel had expected. It helped to have his main character clearly in mind: a mischievous cat that gets two children caught up in some craziness. No other Dr. Seuss character is as recognized as the Cat in the Hat, costumed in a tall red-and-white striped hat and a red bowtie with three, not two, loops. When *The Cat in the Hat* appeared in 1957, according to Morgan, one critic said it was "the most influential first-grader since McGuffey." The McGuffey Readers had been used to teach reading for more than 100 years.

Schools were slower to catch on than the general public. According to Morgan, Geisel explained, "Parents understood better than school people the necessity for this kind of reader." In the beginning, bookstore sales of *The Cat in the Hat* (cover price, $1.95) exceeded 12,000 a month. The success of this new kind of book gave Bennett Cerf's wife,

Did you know...

Ted Geisel struggled and struggled to write his thirteenth children's book. As he looked at the list of 225 words, he cried out to his wife Helen, "There are no adjectives!" He decided he would start by making a title from the first two words that rhymed on the list. Those two words were *cat* and *hat*. *The Cat in the Hat* had a title, but the story took a year to complete. Sometimes he would get so frustrated by the limitations of the word list that he actually threw the manuscript across the room. But he had some fun with it, too, especially in creating a character that was not perfect. He said, as quoted in Charles D. Cohen's book *The Seuss, the Whole Seuss, and Nothing But the Seuss: A Visual Biography of Theodor Seuss Geisel*, "I think a youngster likes to read about someone who is bad for a change—then he realizes he's not the only one who gets into trouble, messes up the house when mother is away."

Eventually all his efforts were rewarded. In its first three years, almost 100 million copies of *The Cat in the Hat* were sold, with translations in Braille, French, Chinese, and Swedish. Geisel never again had to worry about earning a living from his books.

Phyllis, an idea. Why not set up a Random House division just for this kind of reader? She asked Geisel to consider writing four or five more of these beginner books right away, promising that they would not be sold or marketed to compete with his "big books," which did not have the same restrictions as the beginner books. In the spring of 1957, Beginner Books was launched, with Geisel as the president of the division and Helen Geisel as a third partner. This was Geisel's chance to work with new writers and develop a much-needed reading resource for children. Soon a needle-point picture of the Cat was hung at the Geisels' house. According to Fensch, it read: "This cat started a publishing house. No other cat can make this claim."

One of Dr. Seuss's most enduring characters is the Grinch, from How The Grinch Stole Christmas! *Today the word "Grinch" is synonymous with a greedy, selfish miser.*

7

Busy, Busy Dr. Seuss

EVEN AS HE WAS STARTING the new publishing company, Ted Geisel was in the middle of his next "big book." *The Cat in the Hat* was the hardest book he had written thus far, but *How the Grinch Stole Christmas!* was the easiest—except for the ending, which caused him some trouble until he imagined a "roast beast" scene. Seuss's main character was a villain, a creature with a heart "two sizes too small." The author was 53 years old in 1957, so it seems no accident that this bad guy says straightaway: "For fifty-three years I've put up with it now! I MUST stop this Christmas from coming! . . . But HOW?" When asked, Geisel revealed that the idea for this story came from an experience that he had the year before the book was written, while he had been brushing his teeth on the morning of December 26. According to Cohen's biography, he recalled: "I noted a very Grinch-ish countenance in the mirror. It was Seuss! So I wrote the story about my sour friend, the Grinch, to see if I could rediscover something about Christmas that I'd lost."

Ever since the book's publication, the word "Grinch" has stood for a person who is mean-spirited and wants to spoil other people's fun. Geisel must have loved the name, because he had the license plates for his Cadillac changed to spell "GRINCH." The story exposed the greediness of a commercialized Christmas season. In the end, the Grinch himself sums up the moral as he says, "Maybe Christmas doesn't come from a store. Maybe Christmas . . . means a little bit more!"

As sales of *Grinch* multiplied, Geisel got busy with the new enterprise. Phyllis Cerf had created the word list, made up of 379 words from which the writer could use up to 220. Dr. Seuss's next Beginner Book was a sequel to his first. *The Cat in the Hat Comes Back* met a waiting public in 1958. Later that year, the next book in the series arrived—*Yertle the Turtle and Other Stories.* Also that year, Geisel received the Lewis Carroll literary award from the University of Wisconsin. Four more Beginner Books were already underway by other writers and illustrators, including *A Fly Went By* by Mike McClintock, the eager editor who had given Geisel his start in 1937. The Cat from *The Cat in the Hat* became the official logo for the entire series. And Geisel was finally the success he had always hoped to be.

THE BEGINNING OF BEGINNER BOOKS

The five Seuss books that tickled his readers in 1957 through 1959 were just the beginning of what would be the most productive time in Ted Geisel's life. *Happy Birthday to You!*, published in 1959, was for anyone who had a birthday—and that was everyone! Reviewers, as usual, let the world know that dear Dr. Seuss had delivered another wonderful, silly book. While this "big book" was keeping booksellers and librarians busy, Geisel was well underway with his next Beginner Book, *One Fish Two Fish Red Fish Blue Fish*. Limited by 220 words, he again rhymed his way along, delighting readers with fun characters and bright colors. In fact, when he took his final draft to Random House,

Did you know...

Ted Geisel despised racism of all kinds and had been drawing political cartoons about it for many years. He was especially concerned about the segregation issues in schools in the South. In a landmark case, *Brown vs. Board of Education of Topeka*, the National Association for the Advancement of Colored People (NAACP) filed a suit against the Topeka Board of Education because they refused to let Linda Brown attend a white school that was only a few blocks from her house. She was made to walk more than a mile to go to a black school instead. At first, the courts upheld the school board's side. So Geisel wrote a poem that was published in *Redbook* magazine. The poem was titled "The Sneetches." The key idea of his poem (and later of his book) is found in two lines: "And, really, it's sort of a shame/For except for those stars, every Sneetch is the same."

In 1954, the U.S. Supreme Court overturned the Kansas ruling—and segregation of public schools was declared unconstitutional.

he showed up with three crayon pieces to show his editors exactly which three colors he wanted in his book: bright yellow, deep red, and an amazing turquoise. The crayon stubs remained the standard until the author was content that the inks matched exactly. Then he and Helen took a much-deserved vacation.

Beginner Books was an immediate success. By early 1960, the division had sales of more than $1 million. Eighteen different Beginner Books were already available, and plans for many more were already underway. Ready for another challenge, Geisel took a $50 bet from his friend and publisher Bennett Cerf that he could not write a Beginner Book using only 50 words. Geisel took the bet. He then began work on the challenging book that would become *Green Eggs and Ham*.

Slated for sale in fall 1960, *Green Eggs and Ham* was ready for the editors to review in April. After reading the manuscript aloud to the staff at Random House (including Bennett Cerf), everyone knew Geisel had done it again. He won the bet easily. By the end of the year, five of the country's top 16 best-selling children's books were written and illustrated by Dr. Seuss.

Dr. Seuss's *Green Eggs and Ham* became more than the most beloved Seuss book of all time (it has had more than 100 reprintings). It also changed the author's diet. For the rest of his life, Dr. Seuss was served green eggs and ham wherever he went. According to Fensch, his opinion of the food was simple: it was "vile stuff."

Geisel had already written some stories with a political or a social theme, such as *Horton Hears a Who!* and *Yertle the Turtle*. His next book, *The Sneetches and Other Stories* (1961), was a book that clearly spoke to the issue of racism. Some Sneetches had stars on their bellies; some did not.

The starred group felt superior to the other, and there was no getting along between them. In the end, their prejudices were shown for what they were—ridiculous—and both groups learned to live happily together.

Helen had also been busy writing, mostly for Beginner Books, under her maiden name, Helen Palmer. Her book, *A Fish Out of Water*, was published in 1961. That fall, she and Ted traveled to England, where they discovered that Dr. Seuss was not nearly as popular as he was at home. In fact, more of his books were sold for adult reading than for children, and prisoners were even taught to read using them.

Marking the twenty-fifth anniversary of Ted's first book, Random House published *Dr. Seuss's Sleep Book* in 1962. The next year, Dr. Seuss helped new readers by providing them with two new Beginner Books: *Hop on Pop* and

Did you know...

Ted Geisel used exactly 49 different words in *Green Eggs and Ham*. To keep track of this, Ted made huge charts and lists as he worked on the story. The two most-used words were "not" and "I"—each appeared more than 80 times in the book. Only one word in the entire book had more than one syllable—*anywhere*—and he used it only eight times. Most people felt that what made this book so much fun was how Ted turned phrases inside out. "Ham and eggs" became "eggs and ham;" "I am Sam" became "Sam-I-am." Dr. Seuss's *Green Eggs and Ham* became the best-selling, most beloved Seuss book of all time. To date, more than 10 million copies of *Green Eggs and Ham* have been sold.

Dr. Seuss (Theodor Geisel) sits at his desk holding a sketch entitled "Cat Carnival in West Venice—Probably in Italy." Although he preferred dogs to cats in real life, he claimed he had never learned how to draw dogs.

Dr. Seuss's ABC Book. Beginner Books were tagged as "The Simplest Seuss for Youngest Use." He was receiving about 2,000 fan letters a week, many of them from children telling Dr. Seuss how much they liked his rhymes. According to Weidt's biography, a nine-year-old child wrote about one of the books, "It's the funniest book I ever read in nine years." Geisel said the rhymes were so normal for him that he often dreamed in rhyme.

The Geisels traveled to one of their favorite countries in 1964. Australia was a magical place for Ted, and he told people he would move there if he were 20 years younger. Helen enjoyed the trip, too, but returned to California very tired. She had not fully recovered from her previous illness and seemed to become more disabled as each year passed. Still, she continued to write and received good reviews for her next Beginner Book, *Do You Know What I'm Going to Do Next Saturday?* (1963).

Geisel's next Beginner Book was a book of tongue twisters, called *Fox in Socks*. It had a fun "warning" on the cover: "This is a book you READ ALOUD to find out just how smart your tongue is. The first time you read it, don't go fast! This Fox is a tricky fox. He'll try to get your tongue in trouble."

As Dr. Seuss, Geisel was writing both the "big books" for slightly older readers (his next one was *I Had Trouble in Getting to Solla Sollew* in 1965) and the Beginner Books, but he was also writing books under his old pseudonym, Theo LeSieg. These Beginner Books were written, but not illustrated, by Geisel and include *Ten Apples Up On Top!* (1961), *I Wish That I Had Duck Feet* (1965), and *Come on Over to My House* (1966).

TED TRIES TV

In 1966, one of Geisel's old friends from the war films, Chuck Jones, told the author that he wanted to make a television show using one of Dr. Seuss's books. Television in the 1960s was the newest, best source of entertainment, because families could enjoy it in the comfort of their own homes, and color TV was becoming more affordable, too. Still unhappy with the failure from *The 5,000 Fingers of Dr. T*, Geisel was not interested. Helen encouraged her husband to think about Chuck's request, and with her guidance, he listened to his friend.

During the Christmas season of 1966, *How the Grinch Stole Christmas!* glowed in living rooms everywhere, becoming one of America's most beloved television programs ever. (It later became a major motion picture, starring Jim Carrey as the Grinch, in 2000.) Geisel especially loved writing the new parts of the story, in particular the lyrics to "The Grinch Song," that describe the bad guy: "You're cuddly as a cactus/you're as charming as an eel." The biggest challenge in making the show was to stretch a 12-minute story (as it was read from the book) into a 30-minute program. It was a labor of love. The show was the most expensive half-hour TV program that had been made up to that time. It debuted on December 18, 1966, a Sunday evening, at 7:00. As a result of the television version, adults and children renewed their love of Seussian tales and bought his books in record-breaking numbers.

LIFE CHANGES

Sadly, Helen passed away on October 23, 1967, at the age of 69. She had overdosed on painkillers. Helen had been his wife, his friend, his editor, and his best helper for more than 40 years.

Geisel struggled to get on with his work. He had to complete a new kind of book for Beginner Books, one aimed at even younger readers. Bright & Early Books were meant for "pre-readers," children who were just starting to look at books. The first one of its kind was Dr. Seuss's *The Foot Book*, which was published in 1968. Repetition and rhyme made each page easy to remember, and therefore easy to read. His talent sprang to life as he wrote lines like "Left foot / Left foot / Right foot / Right / Feet in the morning / Feet at night." The need to create new books helped Geisel through the grief of losing Helen.

The following summer after Helen's death, Ted married a longtime friend of his and Helen's, Audrey Stone Dimond, who helped him renew his love of travel. They spent much

A still from the animated feature How The Grinch Stole Christmas! *The Christmas special has been an enduring television classic since its debut in 1966.*

of 1969 going from Hawaii, to Japan, to Cambodia, to India, to Israel, to Paris, to London, and finally back to New York. In Japan, Geisel was on hand to celebrate the new Japanese edition of *The Cat in the Hat*. The newlyweds returned to New York just in time for the release of Ted's newest "big book," *I Can Lick 30 Tigers Today! and Other Stories*. It was dedicated to Audrey. The same year (1969) a Theo LeSeig Beginner Book, *My Book About Me*, was also published.

After Ted and Audrey returned to the Geisel home in La Jolla, California, the good Dr. Seuss got back to work right away. Two Seuss books came out in 1970: *I Can Draw It Myself by Me, Myself* (a "big book") and *Mr. Brown Can Moo! Can You?* (a Beginner Book). According to Morgan, the author called the first one "a revolt against coloring books." He followed it with *I Can Write—by Me, Myself* in 1971.

DR. SEUSS GETS SERIOUS

Following his remarriage, Geisel's interest in social and political issues was renewed. Over the past several years, he had watched the beautiful California skies grow grayer and thicker and the land become cluttered with too many buildings. The sadness of seeing the scenery change so much and seeing people disinterested in preserving nature made Ted yearn to travel again. He and Audrey headed for Kenya in September 1970. At the Mt. Kenya Safari Club, he watched African wildlife literally walk past him. One day when he saw a herd of elephants walk by, he was energized with ideas. In one afternoon, he wrote most of his next book, *The Lorax*. The scenery in that book, especially the Truffula trees, resembles the terrain of the Serengheti of Kenya. After several tries, he eventually ended up with a main character who was short and old and had a big mustache. He immediately named him the Lorax because, as he said, according to Morgan, "I looked at the drawing and that's what he was!"

The Lorax addressed the environmental issues of conservation and pollution. In 1971, a book like this was unusual, and some critics did not know what to make of such a serious Seuss. Lady Bird Johnson, a former first lady, knew the book would help raise awareness of environmental issues (one of her pet projects), and Geisel was asked to donate the original art and manuscript to the Lyndon B. Johnson Presidential Library in Austin, Texas. He later said that this "really makes me feel sort of good," as quoted by Morgan. Few people would be surprised to know that *The Lorax* was Geisel's favorite book of all. The next year, *The Lorax* made its appearance as a television special, for which the author won an award at the International Animated Cartoon Festival in Europe. He had already won the coveted 1971 Peabody Award for both *The Grinch* and *Horton Hears a Who!*

Ted continued to work closely with other writers and illustrators at Beginner Books, including Stan and Jan Berenstain, authors of The Berenstain Bears series, and Richard Scarry. A new pseudonym was born in the 1970s, too. Rosetta Stone (named partly for Audrey) became the pen name for the books that Geisel cowrote with Mike Frith, a Beginner Books editor. Over the next several years, a very happy Ted Geisel turned out book after book: *Marvin K. Mooney Will You Please Go Now!* (Bright & Early Books, 1972); *In a People House* (as Theo LeSeig, 1972); *The Many Mice of Mr. Brice* (as Theo LeSeig, 1973); *Did I Ever Tell You How Lucky You Are?* (a "big book," 1973); *The Shape of Me and Other Stuff* (Bright & Early Books, 1973); *Wacky Wednesday* (as Theo LeSeig, 1974); *Great Day for Up* (as Theo LeSeig, 1974); *There's a Wocket in My Pocket!* (as Theo LeSeig, 1974); *Because a Little Bug Went Ka-Choo!* (as Rosetta Stone, 1975); *Oh, The Thinks You Can Think!* (Beginner Books, 1975); and *Would You Rather Be a Bullfrog?* (as Theo LeSeig, 1975).

In 1974, a popular newspaper columnist, Art Buchwald, used one of Dr. Seuss's books to make a political statement. Geisel and Buchwald had met earlier that year at the San Diego Zoo and became fast friends. After Buchwald suggested that Ted write political books, Geisel took out a copy of his book, *Marvin K. Mooney* (a book about a pesky bully), crossed out Marvin's name on each page, inserted another name, sent it to Art, and made history. On July 30, 1974, Art Buchwald printed this in his column:

> Richard M. Nixon, will you please go now!
> The time has come.
> The time is now.
> Just go.
> Go.
> Go! . . .

About a week later, President Nixon resigned after months of scandal associated with his administration. Both Buchwald and Geisel wondered why they had not collaborated sooner.

Unfortunately, Geisel's hard work, late hours, and his heavy smoking began to catch up with him. His first wife, Helen, had tried unsuccessfully for years to get him to quit smoking and to get more rest. According to Morgan, one morning in 1975, he shouted for Audrey, "Am I going blind? I can't focus! Everything is squiggly." His eyesight had been deteriorating over the past few years, and cataracts were to blame. He had initially found a way to work through it by remembering what a certain color "felt" like as he reached for a crayon with a certain nick in it. On top of that, he had also developed glaucoma, a more serious eye disease.

Over the next five years, Geisel endured several surgeries and treatments. Nothing terrified him more as an illustrator than the prospect that he might go blind. As he continued to work on books, he improvised by making his illustrations extra large so they would be easier for him to see. It was difficult for Geisel to see himself in the mirror, so with Audrey's encouragement, he decided to grow a beard so he would not have to shave. He followed his doctors' orders, and his sight improved. In those years, he still wrote and drew with as much talent as ever, finishing *The Cat's Quizzer*, a Beginner Book, for 1976 publication. Then he wrote *I Can Read with My Eyes Shut!* (Beginner Books, 1978) as a tribute to his vision ordeal, and dedicated it to one of his doctors, "David Worthen, E.G.* (*Eye Guy)." He also finished two books as Theo LeSeig between 1974 and 1978: *Hooper Humperdink . . . ? Not Him!* (1976) and *Please Try to Remember the First of Octember* (1977).

In 1979, Theodor Seuss Geisel turned 75. He especially liked the gold cufflinks of the Cat in the Hat he received from a friend, but otherwise was not too excited about turning 75. As quoted by Morgan, he told a reporter, "I meet old, old people, who can scarcely walk, and they say, 'I was brought up on your books.'" Ever young at heart, Ted offered his readers another tongue-twister title in the same year, *Oh Say Can You Say?* Readers also enjoyed his newest Theo LeSeig book, *The Hair Book.* In 1980, Geisel received the Laura Ingalls Wilder Award for his "lasting contributions to children's literature."

The previous five years had been productive, despite the problems with his vision. He had to wear an eye patch for a time. He wrote, telling someone, "For the next several weeks, I'll continue to have double vision, which causes me to burp and bite people and dogs." When the patch was removed, Geisel's vision was completely restored. At 76, Dr. Seuss was at his prime.

Theodor Seuss Geisel, better known as Dr. Seuss, in 1979. Despite health problems in his later years, he continued to be enormously prolific as an author and illustrator.

8

Productive Later Years

WITH HIS EYESIGHT BACK to normal, Ted Geisel began 1981 with the excitement of a child starting something new. His amazing sense of color was as keen as ever, and he helped staff members at Beginner Books put the right colors together for new projects. By summer, he was busy at work on his next Random House "big book," *Hunches in Bunches*. He had not produced a big book since 1973, partly because of his vision trouble and partly because of his activities with Beginner Books. He was ready to get back to the books he loved best.

HEALTH ISSUES AND A BOOK BATTLE

In September, as he was putting the final touches on *Hunches in Bunches*, Geisel asked for some medicine to ease a case of indigestion. Three days later, he still felt the burning in his chest. Audrey called 911, and he was admitted to intensive care. He had suffered a minor heart attack. In general, Geisel was in good health—normal blood pressure and weight—but the doctor told him he had to change one thing about his lifestyle: He would have to quit smoking. Over the years, both Helen and Audrey had done what they could to urge him to quit, but he refused. One evening at a dinner party, Geisel even set a small "No Smoking" sign on fire as a message to his hostess. Now he had no choice. His life was in danger. Not one to do anything like other people, Geisel replaced his cigarettes with a pipe. This pipe, however, did not contain tobacco. It was filled with some peat moss and a few radish seeds. Every time he wanted to smoke, he simply put the pipe in his mouth, pulled out an eyedropper filled with water, and "watered the radishes." Finishing *Hunches in Bunches* was helpful, because it kept his attention on work and not on smoking, but it is interesting that the book begins, "Do you ever sit and fidget / when you don't know what to do?" The author knew exactly what that felt like.

Hunches in Bunches came out in the fall of 1982. That season, Geisel met another popular children's book author and illustrator, Maurice Sendak, creator of *Where the Wild Things Are*. The two men formed an immediate friendship. Usually Geisel was not aware of other children's writers because he was so busy with his own work. He knew Sendak's books, however, and said that if he were a child, those were the books he would read. These authors/illustrators met with a group of fans in San Diego, where they were asked if they liked their characters. According to Morgan, Geisel answered, "If my characters gave me a dinner party, I wouldn't show up." Similarly, Sendak responded, "If we lived with them, we'd be in the madhouse." Later Sendak wrote in his introduction to *The Secret Art of Dr. Seuss*: "The Ted Geisel I knew was that rare amalgamation [mixture] of genial gent and tomcat—a creature content with himself as animal and artist, and one who didn't give a lick or a spit for anyone's opinion, one way or another, of his work. . . . Dr. Seuss was serious about not being serious."

In 1983, Geisel was in the process of finalizing a $10-million contract with the Coleco company, a toy manufacturer. This successful company had created the wildly popular Cabbage Patch Kids dolls, and Coleco's marketing leaders wanted to get Seuss's characters in the marketplace, too. The author and the Coleco people set a date to do the official signing, but other events interrupted. During a regular dental exam, Geisel's dentist noticed a suspicious spot at the base of his tongue. A biopsy showed that it was a kind of cancer that sometimes grew in the mouths of people who smoked. The first doctors Geisel consulted told him that he would have to have a part of his tongue removed in order to save his life. He was upset that his speech would be forever affected, so he went elsewhere for a second opinion. Oncologists, or cancer specialists, at the University of California at San Francisco recommended that he have two procedures: radiation to the area where the tumor was and an implant that would continue delivering low-dosage radiation to the area afterward. The first procedure would affect his voice. He told the doctors to go ahead with the implant, but that he would not agree to the radiation, even though he knew that the implant alone might not destroy the

Dr. Seuss signs a copy of The Butter Battle Book *during a party celebrating his eightieth birthday at the New York Public Library in 1984.* The Butter Battle Book *was written in response to the escalating arms race between the United States and the Soviet Union.*

cancer completely. Two weeks later, after the implant, he returned with Audrey to La Jolla.

Geisel had seldom been ill, so he was frustrated that his body was interfering with his work. He had a new passion burning in his mind, and a book was already "cooking" in his imagination. Not since *The Lorax* had he written a book with a political theme. In the 1970s and 1980s, the United States and the former Soviet Union were competing with each other to create bigger and more effective nuclear weapons, just in case the other would attack. This "arms race" scared people. Large areas of the planet could be destroyed within minutes if these weapons were ever used. Geisel, too, was concerned. And he had something to say about it. Respected by the people at Random House as the "most important book Dr. Seuss has ever created," *The Butter Battle Book* was also his most controversial one. The author was passionate about his message, and for the first time, all the words came first, before any of the drawings. The book came out on Geisel's eightieth birthday in 1984. It brought immediate and mixed responses—some people thought the subject was too frightening for children, while others thought it was the right time to address the issue. *The Butter Battle Book* appeared on the *New York Times* best-seller list for six months—on the *adult* list. The open ending kept discussions going:

> "Grandpa!" I shouted. "Be careful! Oh, gee!
> Who's going to drop it?
> Will *you* . . . ? Or will *he* . . . ?"
> "Be patient," said Grandpa. "We'll see.
> We will see . . ."

Regardless of people's opinions about this book, Ted Geisel won a special Pulitzer Prize in 1984 for his lifetime of contributions to children's literature. He and Audrey were invited to the White House to meet President and Mrs. Ronald Reagan. According to Morgan, like the wily Cat in the Hat, the author could not resist whispering to Audrey, "Now seven presidents have met me."

ON GETTING OLD AND SAYING GOOD-BYE

Despite all of Ted Geisel's success, both financially and professionally, he and Audrey lived simply. They owned one car, a silver Cadillac with "GRINCH" always on the license plates. They answered their own phone. Geisel did not give in to the computer age, and, in fact, never even owned an electric typewriter. Rather than spending money on luxuries (even buying a new suit was unusual for the author), the Geisels gave money to good causes, such as universities and hospitals. They also bought land around them, hoping to help preserve the area from development.

Geisel's battle with cancer continued. The tumor in his mouth was not fully destroyed by the implant, and doctors soon discovered that the disease was spreading into his throat and neck. Still, he kept a positive attitude about his life. At 82, he said, "I surf as much as I always have!

Did you know...

As soon as Ted Geisel finished *The Butter Battle Book*, he said, as quoted by Morgan, "I have no idea if this is an adult book for children or a children's book for adults." The serious subject of nuclear war made many people at Random House nervous, and they had their own mini-war about what to do with the book. Some wanted to change the title to *The Yook and the Zooks*. Some wanted a different cover from the cheerleader image Geisel had given them. In the end, all of the author's original ideas won. *The Butter Battle Book* was strongly endorsed by another great author/illustrator: Maurice Sendak. Later, in 1990, the book was made into an animated television special. "Right after that," Ted said proudly, according to Morgan, "the U.S.S.R. began falling apart."

I climb Mount Everest as much as I always have!" Of course, he had never done either, so he was not lying. His sense of humor and the love of his fans kept him going. In 1985, he was given an honorary degree from Princeton University. As he stood before the graduating class, all of the students stood up and loudly recited word-for-word the book *Green Eggs and Ham*. Dr. Seuss was deeply touched.

Not one to waste any of his experiences, Geisel started writing a book about growing old. *You're Only Old Once!* was subtitled *A Book for Obsolete Children*, and it made fun of doctors and hospitals, especially the high cost of medical care—things he knew a lot about. Although the children's book division worked on the book with Geisel, it was the adult division that worked to sell it—to adults, of course. This was Geisel's forty-fifth book, and it appeared on his eighty-second birthday in 1986. During a book signing at a New York bookstore, he joked as he looked at the never-ending line of 1,300 fans who were waiting for his autograph. "Thank God," he said, as quoted by Weidt, "my name isn't Henry Wadsworth Longfellow!"

Later that year, he and Audrey returned to Springfield, Massachusetts, for a Dr. Seuss exhibition and to see his old neighborhood once more. They walked down Mulberry Street, and the townspeople were overjoyed to see their native son return. Two hundred schoolchildren greeted him, flying a banner that read: "And to think that we saw him on Mulberry Street!" He held the children's hands and wiped away tears as they recited lines from *Green Eggs and Ham*. Ted took Audrey to his old home, where he was welcomed to come inside. He showed his wife the rooms where he had punched pencil holes in the walls and had sketched funny-looking animals on the wallpaper, long since covered over.

By 1987, Geisel's health was declining. He kept working, however, this time on a Beginner Book called *I Am Not Going to Get Up Today!* He was only able to work on the words, and had another artist, James Stevenson, do the illustrations. Knowing he was reaching the end of his life, Ted turned his attention to revising some of his older books so they could continue being published for children. *Mulberry Street* needed the most work because it had included some racial stereotypes, which at the time the book was first published were not considered inappropriate. He had drawn a Chinese man with yellow skin and a pigtail hairstyle. "That's the way things were fifty years ago," Ted explained, according to Morgan. "In later editions, I refer to him as a Chinese man. I have taken the color out of the gentleman and removed the pigtail and now he looks like an Irishman."

One other important change appeared in *The Lorax.* The first edition had included the line: "I hear things are just as bad up in Lake Erie." Some scientists who were involved in the cleanup project for Lake Erie actually wrote to Dr. Seuss, asking him if he might consider changing that reference since Lake Erie was now much cleaner. The line was later completely deleted from the book. Not all changes that had been requested by readers were made, however. Two brothers from New Jersey, David and Bob Grinch, wrote to ask Geisel to change the name of the Grinch, because they were being harassed. According to Morgan, the author wrote back, letting the boys know that the Grinch was really a hero because, "he starts out as a villain, but it's not how you start out that counts. It's what you are at the finish." The Grinch stayed.

Eight-hour workdays continued for Ted Geisel until the end of his life. In 1989, he immersed himself in what he knew would be his last book, *Oh, the Places You'll Go!* Somehow he found the strength to both write and illustrate this last book. In 1990, it became a beloved addition to the Dr. Seuss collection of books.

Over the years at La Jolla, Geisel had loved to give away books and autographs to support children's organizations, schools, and zoos. When the San Diego Youth and Community Services group asked for donations for a fund-raising auction, the rock group Aerosmith agreed to send in a signed guitar if Dr. Seuss would donate some autographed books, which he did. Geisel donated money to some La Jolla High School science students who needed help getting to a Science Olympiad with their project called "The Scrambler." The invention was used to launch an egg 10 meters (32 feet) into a wall, creating a scrambled egg inside. According to Weidt, Geisel's check arrived with a note attached: "Scrambling has always been my favorite Olympic sport."

As Geisel grew weaker, his wife, family, and friends gathered around to spend the remaining time with the man they loved. His close friend and chief biographer, Neil Morgan, asked him what message he would like to leave behind. His answer: "I always tell myself: 'You can do better than this.' The best slogan I can think of to leave with the U.S.A. would be: 'We can do and we've *got* to do better than this.'" And he was not talking only to children this time. He was talking to everyone.

In the end, Geisel refused to return to a hospital. He stayed at his home with Audrey, sleeping more and more as days went by. On September 24, 1991, at about 10:00 P.M., Theodor Seuss Geisel died at the age of 87. Nearby was the drawing board where characters came to life from the hands and mind of Dr. Seuss, characters that will never grow old.

A photo of the Dr. Seuss National Memorial Sculpture Garden at the Springfield Museum in Springfield, Massachusetts. Lark Grey Dimond-Cates, a sculptor who is also Geisel's stepdaughter, created the garden's bronze sculptures, including the one seen above.

9

A Lasting Legacy

How did it get so late so soon?
It's night before it's afternoon.
December is here before it's June.
My goodness how the time has flewn.
How did it get so late so soon?

—Dr. Seuss

THEODOR SEUSS GEISEL has no marked grave for fans to visit. Instead, fans can "visit" him by sitting with any one of the 48 books he created. Upon his death, the editors of *Time* honored Dr. Seuss by saying he was "one of the last doctors to make house calls—some 200 million of them in

20 languages." *USA Today* offered these words about the death of Dr. Seuss:

> This is no time for fun,
> This is no time for play,
> Dr. Seuss is no more,
> It's a sad, sad, sad day.

Since his death, tributes have abounded. Thousands of pieces of his original work have been donated to universities across the country. Some of these can be seen at the University of California at Los Angeles (UCLA) and the University of California at San Diego, where Audrey Geisel dedicated the Geisel Room in a wing of the library in 1993. Springfield, Massachusetts, Geisel's hometown, opened the Dr. Seuss National Memorial in June 2002. Five sculptures created by Audrey Geisel's daughter and Ted's stepdaughter, Lark Grey Dimond-Cates, highlight the best of Dr. Seuss's works. These sculptures include Yertle the Turtle in the Yertle Garden, a 14-foot-high (4.2-meter-high) Horton the elephant in Horton Court, a four-foot-tall (1.2-meter-tall) Lorax on a tree stump that reads "Unless," and, of course, Dr. Seuss himself at his drawing board with the Cat in Hat beside him.

Many people are not aware of the National Aeronautical and Space Administration's (NASA) tribute to the good doctor. In 1994, their engineers designed a deep-space unmanned craft dubbed DRSEUS (Data Relay Solar Electric Utility Spacecraft). To them, it was known simply as "Dr. Seuss."

On what would have been Ted Geisel's one-hundredth birthday, March 2, 2004, the United States Postal Service dedicated a commemorative postage stamp that featured a photo of Theodor Seuss Geisel and six of his beloved illustrated characters, including the Grinch and the Cat in the Hat. One hundred seventy-two million stamps were printed, and collectible framed prints were sold in 2004.

Literary awards honoring Geisel's vision and leadership in children's literature were created. Random House Books for Young Readers created a Dr. Seuss Picture Book Award for a first-time author and illustrator, offering a $25,000 prize and a guaranteed book contract, in memory of one of the publishing house's most beloved authors and illustrators. In 2004, the American Library Association (ALA) established the annual Theodor Seuss Geisel Award, which is given to "the author(s) and illustrator(s) of the most distinguished American book for beginning readers published in the United States." The winner(s) receive a bronze medal with Geisel's image on it. The first medal was presented in 2006, and it is one of the most prized children's book awards in the United States.

Although the name "Ted Geisel" may not be familiar to some, the name "Dr. Seuss" lights the eyes of millions of fans, young and old, around the word. For more than 70 years, this doctor has had just the right prescription for making reading fun.

CHRONOLOGY

1904 Theodor Seuss Geisel is born on March 2 in Springfield, Massachusetts.

1906 His sister, Henrietta Geisel, is born.

1907 Henrietta Geisel dies.

1921 Enters Dartmouth College.

1925 Graduates Dartmouth College; goes to England and enters Oxford College; meets Helen Palmer.

1926 Travels through Europe with his family.

1927 Returns to the United States; his first cartoon is published in the *Saturday Evening Post*; he moves to New York City and marries Helen Palmer.

1928 Starts work illustrating ads for Flit insecticide.

1931 His mother, Henrietta Geisel, dies.

1937 Publishes his first book *And to Think That I Saw It on Mulberry Street!*

1938 Switches publishers from Vanguard Press to Random House.

1941 Moves to Hollywood during World War II to join the Signal Corps.

1945 Goes to Germany to work on *Your Job in Germany* film; his sister, Marnie Geisel, dies.

1948 Moves to La Jolla, California, with Helen.

1954 Helen is diagnosed with Guillain-Barré syndrome.

1956 Receives an honorary doctorate from his alma mater, Dartmouth College.

1957 Becomes president of Random House's Beginner Books division.

1966 Works on TV adaptation of *How the Grinch Stole Christmas!* with Chuck Jones.

1967 Works on TV adaptation of *Horton Hears a Who!*; Helen Geisel dies.

1968 Marries Audrey Stone Dimond.

1975 Undergoes treatment for glaucoma.

1980 Eyesight restored.

1983 Diagnosed with cancer and undergoes treatment.

1985 Receives an honorary degree from Princeton University.

1991 Dies on September 24.

WORKS BY DR. SEUSS

1937 *And to Think That I Saw It on Mulberry Street!*

1938 *The 500 Hats of Bartholomew Cubbins*

1939 *The Seven Lady Godivas*
    The King's Stilts

1940 *Horton Hatches the Egg*

1947 *McElligot's Pool*

1948 *Thidwick the Big-Hearted Moose*

1949 *Bartholomew and the Oobleck*

1950 *If I Ran the Zoo*

1951 *Gerald McBoing Boing* (cartoon film)

1952 *The 5,000 Fingers of Dr. T* (cartoon film)

1953 *Scrambled Eggs Super!*

1954 *Horton Hears a Who!*

1955 *On Beyond Zebra*

1956 *If I Ran the Circus*

1957 *How the Grinch Stole Christmas!*; *The Cat in the Hat**

1958 *The Cat in the Hat Comes Back**; *Yertle the Turtle and Other Stories*

1959 *Happy Birthday to You!*

1960 *Green Eggs and Ham**; *One Fish Two Fish Red Fish Blue Fish**

1961 *The Sneetches and Other Stories*; *Ten Apples Up on Top!***

1962 *Dr. Seuss's Sleep Book*

1963 *Hop on Pop**; *Dr. Seuss's ABC**

1965 *Fox in Socks**; *I Had Trouble Getting to Solla Sollew*; *I Wish That I Had Duck Feet***

1966 *Come Over to My House***; *How the Grinch Stole Christmas!* (television special)

1967 *The Cat in the Hat Song Book*; *Horton Hears a Who!* (television special)

1968 *The Foot Book*; The Eye Book***

1969 *I Can Lick 50 Tigers Today! and Other Stories; My Book about Me*

1970 *I Can Draw It Myself; Mr. Brown Can Moo! Can You?**

1971 *I Can Write—by Me, Myself**; The Lorax*

1972 *In a People House**; Marvin K. Mooney Will You Please Go Now!*

1973 *The Many Mice of Mr. Brice**; Did I Ever Tell You How Lucky You Are?; The Shape of Me and Other Stuff**

1974 *There's a Wocket in My Pocket*; Great Day for Up*

1975 *Because a Little Bug Went Ka-Choo!**; Oh, the Thinks You Can Think*; Would You Rather Be a Bullfrog?***

1976 *Hooper Humperdink . . .? Not Him!**; The Cat's Quizzer**

1977 *Please Try to Remember the First of October**; Halloween Is Grinch Night* (television special).

1978 *I Can Read with My Eyes Shut!**

1979 *Oh Say Can You Say?**

1980 *Maybe You Should Fly a Jet! Maybe You Should Be a Vet!***

1981 *The Tooth Book***

1982 *Hunches in Bunches; The Grinch Grinches the Cat in the Hat* (television special)

1984 *The Butter Battle Book*

1986 *You're Only Old Once!*

1987 *I Am Not Going to Get Up Today!**

1990 *Oh, The Places You'll Go!*

1991 *Six by Seuss: A Treasury of Dr. Seuss Classics*

1995 *Daisy-Head Mayzie; The Secret Art of Dr. Seuss*

1996 *My Many-Colored Days; A Hatful of Seuss*

1997 *Seuss-isms: Wise and Witty Prescriptions for Living from the Good Doctor*

1998 *Hooray for Diffendoofer Day* (completed by Jack Prelutsky using Ted Geisel's notes)

   *   Indicates a Beginner or Bright & Early Book.

 **   Indicates a Theo LeSeig or other pseudonym used.

POPULAR BOOKS

THE CAT IN THE HAT

The story of a mischievous cat who transforms a dull, rainy after-noon into a crazy adventure for two children and a fish while their mother is out.

GREEN EGGS AND HAM

Sam, the main character, tries every way possible to convince his friend to eat green eggs and ham—in a house, with a mouse, in a box, with a fox, with a goat, on a boat—until his friend finally breaks down and tries them, only to discover that he actually likes them.

HORTON HATCHES THE EGG

A kind elephant named Horton sits on an egg while its mother, a lazy bird named Mayzie, takes a break. Little does Horton know that Mayzie has gone on vacation in Palm Springs. He waits through a freezing winter and suffers from the insults of his friends to pro-tect the egg.

HOW THE GRINCH STOLE CHRISTMAS!

The mean and awful Grinch comes up with a devious plan to pre-vent Christmas from coming to the Whos down in Whoville by dressing up as Santa Claus and stealing their presents, but in the process learns the true meaning of Christmas.

THE LORAX

Long ago, Once-ler, a faceless villain, comes upon a wonderful place filled with wondrous Truffula Trees, Swomee-Swans, Brown Bar-ba-loots, and Humming-Fishes. Enchanted by the beauty of the Truffula Tree tufts, he greedily chops them down to produce and mass-market Thneeds.

POPULAR CHARACTERS

THE CAT IN THE HAT
The Cat is the sly character who mysteriously appears one day and entertains two kids with his "tricks" and "games," though their fish is suspicious of the Cat's intentions.

HORTON
He is the elephant who helps an irresponsible bird by sitting in her nest until her egg hatches.

THE GRINCH
The Grinch is Dr. Seuss's own Ebenezer Scrooge who tries to ruin Christmas for the town of Whoville by stealing all their gifts—only to discover that the town still celebrates as happily as they would have even if their presents were not stolen.

THE LORAX
The Lorax tries to save the Truffula Forest from the Once-ler's greedy actions.

SAM
He is the persistent character who wants a grumpy man to eat green eggs and ham . . . until finally the man agrees and discovers he actually likes them.

MAJOR AWARDS

1974 Geisel wins the Los Angeles County Library Association Award.

1976 He wins Outstanding California Author Award from the California Association of Teachers of English.

1980 He wins Laura Ingalls Wilder Award from the American Library Association.

1982 Geisel wins the Regina Medal from the Catholic Library Association and a Special Award for Distinguished Service to Children from the National Association of Elementary School Principals.

1984 Geisel wins the Pulitzer Prize.

1986 He is named a New York Public Library Literary Lion.

2006 American Library Association awards its first Theodor Seuss Geisel Award to the most distinguished book for beginning readers.

BIBLIOGRAPHY

Addabbo, Grace. "Celebrating Seuss." *Parents Magazine* 2004. Available online. URL: http://www.parents.com/fun/entertainment/books/dr-seuss/

"American Occupation of Japan, 1945–1952, The." Asia for Educators, Columbia University. Available online. URL: http://afe.easia.columbia.edu/.

Bandler, Michael J. "Seuss on the Loose." *Parents*, September 1987.

Cerf, Bennett. *At Random: The Reminiscences of Bennett Cerf.* New York: Random House, 1977.

Cohen, Charles D. *The Seuss, the Whole Seuss, and Nothing But the Seuss: A Visual Biography of Theodor Seuss Geisel.* New York: Random House, 2004.

"Coming June 1, 2002: The Dr. Seuss National Memorial!" Springfield Museums Homepage. Available online. URL: http://www.springfieldmuseums.org/.

Corliss, Richard. "That Old Feeling: Seuss on First." *Time*, March 2, 2004.

"Fallen Hero: Charles Lindbergh in the 1940s." *American Experience.* PBS Online. Available online. URL: http://www.pbs.org/wgbh/amex/lindbergh/sfeature/fallen.html.

Fensch, Thomas. *The Man Who Was Dr. Seuss.* Woodlands, Tex.: New Century Books, 2000.

"Holiday Shipping Made Easy with The Cat in the Hat." Press release, No. 082. United States Postal Service, October 31, 2003.

Kerr, Austin. "Temperance and Prohibition." The Ohio State University College of Humanities. Available online. URL: http://prohibition.osu.edu/.

Marcus, Leonard S. *Minders of Make-Believe: Idealists, Entrepreneurs, and the Shaping of American Children's Literature.* Boston: Houghton Mifflin Company, 2008.

McElmeel, Sharron L. *100 Most Popular Picture Book Authors and Illustrators.* Englewood, Colo.: Libraries Unlimited, Inc., 2000.

Minear, Richard H. *Dr. Seuss Goes to War: The World War II Editorial Cartoons of Theodor Seuss Geisel.* New York: The Free Press, 1999.

Morgan, Judith, and Neil Morgan. *Dr. Seuss and Mr. Geisel.* New York: Da Capo Press, 1995.

Nel, Philip. *Dr Seuss: American Icon.* New York: Continuum International Publishing Group, 2004.

"New Magazines." *1930's Media.* Gale Cengage, 1995.

"Overview." *1920's Media.* Gale Cengage, 1996.

Seuss, Dr., and Audrey S. Geisel. *The Secret Art of Dr. Seuss.* New York: Random House, 1995.

"Smart Magazines, The." *1910's Media.* Gale Cengage, 1996.

"Sputnik and the Dawn of the Space Age." NASA.gov. Available online. URL: http://history.nasa.gov/sputnik/.

Sullivan, Robert. "Oh, the Places He Went!" *Dartmouth Alumni Magazine,* Winter 1991.

"Theodor Geisel." Available online. URL: http://www.english.uiuc.edu/martindale/magazine_illustrations.htm.

"Theodore Seuss Geisel Award." American Library Association/Association for Library Service to Children. Available online. URL: http://www.ala.org/ala/mgrps/divs/alsc/awardsgrants/bookmedia/geiselaward/geiselabout/index.cfm.

"Theodor Seuss Geisel Honored by U.S. Postal Service: New Stamp Dedicated." Press release, No. 04-016. United States Postal Service, March 2, 2004.

Theodor Seuss Geisel: The Early Works of Dr. Seuss, Volume 1. West Carrollton, Ohio: Checker Book Publishing Group, 2005.

Theodor Seuss Geisel: The Early Works of Dr. Seuss, Volume 2. West Carrollton, Ohio: Checker Book Publishing Group, 2006.

Weidt, Maryann N. *Oh, The Places He Went.* Minneapolis: Carolrhoda Books, Inc., 1994.

Zielinski, Linda, and Stan Zielinski. *Children's Picturebook Price Guide.* Park City, Utah: Flying Moose Books, 2006.

FURTHER READING

Books

Geisel, Audrey. *The Secret Art of Dr. Seuss*. New York: Random House, 1995.

Geisel, Theodor. *Dr. Seuss from Then to Now: A Catalogue of the Retrospective Exhibition*. New York: Random House, 1987.

———. *Theodor Seuss Geisel: The Early Works, Volume 1*. West Carrollton, Ohio: Checker Book Publishing, 2005.

———. *Dr. Seuss Goes to War: The World War II Editorial Cartoons of Theodor Seuss Geisel*. Edited by Richard Minnear. New York: New Press, 2001.

———. *The Tough Coughs As He Ploughs the Dough: Early Writings and Cartoons by Dr. Seuss*. New York: Morrow, 1987.

Web Sites

The Dr. Seuss National Memorial Sculpture Garden
http://www.catinthehat.org

The Exclusive Publisher of Dr. Seuss's Artworks
http://www.drseussart.com

The Official Dr. Seuss Web Site
http://www.seussville.com

PICTURE CREDITS

INDEX

ABOUT THE CONTRIBUTOR

TANYA ANDERSON is a children's book writer, editor, and conference speaker. She taught history and English for 12 years before moving into the field of publishing. Ms. Anderson was the editorial director of Darby Creek Publishing from 2002–2009, and previously worked in a variety of editorial positions at Willowisp Press/Pages Publishing Group, *Guideposts for Teens*, and SRA/McGraw-Hill. Today she writes, edits, and packages books at School Street Media, her very own company. Ms. Anderson read Dr. Seuss books to her three sons, now grown up, and is kind of proud of the fact that she was born the same year as the Cat in the Hat and the Grinch.